OPPORTUNITIES

in

Dental Care Careers

OPPORTUNITIES

in

Dental Care
Careers

REVISED EDITION

BONNIE L. KENDALL

McGraw·Hill

New York   Chicago   San Francisco   Lisbon   London   Madrid   Mexico City
Milan   New Delhi   San Juan   Seoul   Singapore   Sydney   Toronto

Library of Congress Cataloging-in-Publication Data

Kendall, Bonnie L.
　　　Opportunities in dental care careers / by Bonnie Kendall. — Rev. ed.
　　　　　p.　　cm.
　　　ISBN 0-07-145869-7 (alk. paper)
　　　1. Dentistry—Vocational guidance.　　I. Title.

　　RK60.K44　　2006
　　617.6'0071—dc22　　　　　　　　　　　　　　2005024495

1 2 3 4 5 6 7 8 9 0　 DOC/DOC　 0 9 8 7 6

ISBN 0-07-145869-7

Interior design by Rattray Design

McGraw-Hill books are available at special quantity discounts to use as premiums and sales promotions, or for use in corporate training programs. For more information, please write to the Director of Special Sales, Professional Publishing, McGraw-Hill, Two Penn Plaza, New York, NY 10121-2298. Or contact your local bookstore.

This book is printed on acid-free paper.

Contents

Early dental practices. Founder of modern dentistry. Dentistry in the United States. Twentieth century to today. Orthodontia. Veterinary dentistry. The first formal dental school. History of dental hygiene. History of dental assisting. History of dental laboratory technology.

What a dentist does. Job outlook. Salaries for dentists. Areas of specialty.

PREFACE

DENTISTRY IS THE treatment and care of the teeth and associated oral structures. Those working in the field are primarily concerned with tooth decay; disease of the supporting structures, such as the gums; and improper positioning of the teeth. Dentists often practice in specialized fields: oral surgery, orthodontics (corrective dentistry), periodontics (diseases of the gums), prosthodontics (partial or total tooth replacement), endodontics (treatment of dental pulp chamber and canals), and pedodontics (dental problems of children), to name just a few. The field is indeed vast, and it is full of opportunities.

Today, in part because of fluorinated water, proper oral hygiene, and faithful visits to a competent dentist, many children rarely get cavities, and many adults are unlikely to end up with dentures. But this does not mean that dentistry isn't still a viable career. On the contrary, dentists are very much in demand. The main difference between the dentists of today and those of yesterday is that today's dentists tend to work with healthier teeth.

There are several reasons for the improved state of dental health. For one, the science of dentistry over recent decades has made enormous changes in the delivery and types of treatment. Years past, a dentist worked alone. But today the dental office is staffed with a team of dental professionals that generally includes, in addition to the dentist, a dental hygienist, dental assistant, sometimes a laboratory assistant, and a receptionist. Also, new specialties have emerged and established specialties continue to grow, which add to the services this field has to offer.

Concurrent with this change in dental office makeup is the fact that today people care more about their teeth than ever before. Over the years, the emphasis in dentistry has become one of prevention. As we take better care of our teeth, under the guidance of the dentist and his or her dental team, a visit to the dentist's office—though not necessarily a pleasant experience—need not be a torturous ordeal.

Modern techniques and materials at the dentist's disposal help make teeth stronger, more attractive, and apt to last a lifetime. Dentistry today is not just a matter of "pulling teeth." It involves diagnosing, treating, and preventing diseases of the teeth, gums, and jaws; cleaning teeth; and teaching patients about proper oral hygiene as well as helping them establish good nutritional eating habits to help keep teeth and gums strong.

In addition to prevention, today's focus is often on cosmetic dentistry. People not only want to feel good, they want to look good, too. Many dentists provide a range of services, from filling cavities to whitening and capping teeth. It's easy to see why a career in this field can offer so many interesting options to those attracted to it.

If you decide to enter the field of dental care, you will join a prestigious group of more than four million people in health careers. You will be concerned with much more than the state of the patient's mouth. You will be actively involved with the health care of your patients. You will be concerned with the education of patients in preventive dentistry. You will be involved with children, adults, elderly patients, and patients with special needs. You will work long hours in training and on the job, but you will have security in your profession and pride in your accomplishments.

If you're interested in any of the various jobs the field of dentistry has to offer, *Opportunities in Dental Care Careers* will give you a clear picture of what to expect as you pursue a career as a dentist, dental hygienist, laboratory technician, endodontist, orthodontist, pediatric dentist, or any of the many other areas there are to choose from. You'll also learn what it's like to deal with different patient populations, how much money you can expect to make over your years of practice, the educational requirements of your area of interest, and the associations and other professional organizations that are there to support you. Good luck as you find your place in this exciting and rewarding profession!

ACKNOWLEDGMENTS

Previous editions of this book could not have been written without the help of those at the American Dental Association and the *Journal of the American Dental Association,* who supplied valuable facts and figures about the profession of dentistry. These individuals are committed to furthering the field of dentistry.

1

THE INCREDIBLE HISTORY
OF DENTISTRY

TOOTH DECAY AND diseases involving the teeth and gums have been around since the beginning of mankind. Archaeologists have uncovered the skulls of Cro-Magnon people showing signs of serious tooth decay. The earliest known writing about tooth disease was an ancient Sumerian text that dates to about 5000 B.C. accusing "tooth worms" of burrowing into teeth thus forming the characteristic holes of tooth decay—a superstition that persisted through the Middle Ages in Asia, the Middle East, and Europe. Although the high technology of modern dentistry is a fairly recent phenomenon, there is evidence of efforts to treat tooth decay even as far back as 2700 B.C. in ancient China and Egypt. This chapter explores the fascinating history of dentistry—from the truth about George Washington's false teeth to the inventor of floss and more in between!

Early Dental Practices

Many dental procedures have existed for thousands of years, even though dentistry was not recognized as a separate and distinct profession until the eighteenth century. Some practices go back to the Egyptian empire of 2000 B.C., where medicine was a profession in which a physician's work was limited to one area of the body, including focusing on the teeth and mouth. Archaeologists uncovered a jaw in Egypt that had two holes drilled into it, presumably to drain an abscessed tooth. Ancient papyrus records show that Egyptians had remedies for toothaches, such as stone powder, ocher (iron ore), and honey. A tooth powder for "strengthening" teeth was described as resin, ocher, and malachite (a copper mixture). Ancient Egyptian physicians, while they treated diseased teeth, practiced little restorative dentistry except to use wires to secure loosened teeth. Oral hygiene was a common practice of the time, as evidenced by the often occurring hieroglyph, or sign, for "washing the mouth" on papyrus records.

In ancient India and China, groups of physicians made up a professional class and received training as students. While there is no evidence during this period to show whether parents were as rigorous as today's parents about encouraging their kids to brush after every meal, medical writings of the time recommended that people use a toothbrush. The Chinese are thought to have invented the toothbrush using the stiff hairs from cold climate pigs' necks in creating their brushes. The ancient Egyptian toothbrush was a twig with its end frayed into bristles. People at this time used toothpicks to remove food from between their teeth and scraped their tongues with metal scrapers to remove debris.

Chinese physicians practiced acupuncture (application of very thin needles to specific points on the body) in treating nearly every disease, including diseases of the mouth. Acupuncture is still practiced in China today. It has also enjoyed a growing popularity in the United States, embraced by the general population and health care providers alike. While acupuncture is not often used in dental practices in the United States, it is generally accepted to be beneficial in relieving stress, tension, and pain.

Decorating teeth was a common practice both in China and in Central and South America. The Chinese used gold to make covers for their teeth. The Aztec and Mayan Indians inserted semiprecious stones such as turquoise and jade into their teeth. This practice survived to modern times, when it became popular in the 1980s and '90s in U.S. hip-hop culture.

Around the world, remedies for toothache consisted of medicines made from crushing and mixing a variety of plants. Cloves, pepper, cinnamon, poppy seeds, ginger, copal (resin from trees), mint, and tobacco were often the plants of choice. Many of these treatments were combined with special incantations, or poems and songs, to make the remedy more effective.

Greek-Roman Dentistry

The Greek physician Hippocrates, who lived about the fifth century B.C., raised the practice of medicine to a higher level. During his lifetime, he made extensive studies of the human body and its workings and established a school based on his prolific writings and teachings. While Hippocrates covered a range of topics in his writing, he devoted nearly thirty-two paragraphs in his books to dental treatment. In addition, he even devised a numbering system for teeth.

Hippocrates advised extraction of teeth only if they were both decayed and weak. For decayed teeth, he recommended that physicians insert a red-hot wire into the tooth to cauterize the decay. Physicians treated fractures or breaks in the jaw by repositioning the bone and holding it in place with wire until the jaw healed. To restore lost teeth, they drilled teeth and passed wires through the holes and wound the wire around the natural teeth. This was all in a time before strong painkillers were invented!

Contact with Greek civilization helped carry dental knowledge into the Roman Empire. Three groups of practitioners dealt with problems of teeth: the regular physician, the physician specializing in dentistry, and the technician. These dental practitioners extracted teeth with forceps made of iron, which resembled today's pliers. They used small drills to relieve pressure inside a tooth and small sticks of mastic wood (from an evergreen tree) to clean teeth. Finally, they ground tooth powders from fine pumice, eggshell, and animal horn.

Restorative dentistry was largely learned from the work of the Etruscans in central Italy. The Etruscans made numerous crowns and bridges out of gold, and today you can see these displayed in Italian museums. Then as now, crowns were used to replace and cover missing portions of teeth, and bridges were artificial teeth attached at either end to natural teeth. The Etruscans used gold bands to hold in place the replacement teeth that had been removed from other humans or calves. In the prosperous days of the Roman Empire, artificial teeth became valued as a way to improve one's appearance, and many restorative procedures were developed. Like many Greek and Roman discoveries, this important knowledge was lost as the Roman Empire disappeared, and they had to be "reinvented" in later days.

Dentistry in the Middle Ages

Many of the tools and techniques that were developed in early civilizations improved little during the Middle Ages. In fact, this was a time when dentistry and medicine made few advances. Only the very wealthy received dental care of any competence with regularity. For the wealthy, physicians and surgeons would make home visits to either excise, or pull, teeth or relieve pressure by "drilling" them with a pointed metal instrument that they rubbed vigorously between their hands. The holes were then packed with a soft material, similar to today's methods. Monks in monasteries mainly preserved the knowledge of dentistry.

The chief dental remedy for the majority of the people in Europe during the Middle Ages was the removal of teeth. Even Queen Elizabeth I (1533–1603) is said to have filled the holes in her mouth left from extracted teeth with cloth when she went out in public to improve her appearance. "Barber surgeons," who not only cut hair, but also pulled teeth, performed minor surgery, and applied leeches for medicinal purposes, usually did tooth excision. For the poorest people, self-taught drifters would go from town to town and ply their trade at markets. They often wore a necklace of teeth to proclaim their trade, and they bragged about the painlessness of their methods, although this was unlikely to be the case.

Revival of Scientific Thought

Based on writings of the time, by the end of the Middle Ages in Italy, we know that physicians filled teeth using gold leaf. This was the beginning of a time in which science and medicine began, once again, to make tremendous discoveries.

In the early sixteenth century, interest was rekindled in scientific thought and methods. The study of the anatomy of the human body led to new discoveries about the mouth and teeth. Andreas Vesalius (1514–64), a Flemish anatomist, described with some accuracy the parts of the teeth. A French dental pioneer, Ambroise Pare (1510–90), described methods for transplanting teeth, repairing fractures, and removing teeth. He recommended dental substitutes of bone held in place with wire and filled teeth with lead and cork when treating dental caries. The Dutch inventor of the microscope, Anton van Leeuwenhoek (1632–1723), was the first to see the organisms that are found in the mouth. An Italian anatomist, Bartolommeo Eustachius (1683–1758), illustrated the development of teeth in all phases, and he wrote one of the first books entirely devoted to dentistry. The work of all these scientists became known and could be shared with others because of the invention of printing and the fairly easy accessibility to their books.

Founder of Modern Dentistry

Pierre Fauchard (1678–1761), a French physician, is widely considered to be the founder of modern dentistry. Fauchard practiced in Paris and began his training with a surgeon in the royal navy. His outstanding contribution to dentistry was his two-volume, 848-page book published in 1728. This book on dental information, known in English as *The Surgeon Dentist: A Treatise on Teeth*, proved to be an authoritative guide for more than a hundred years. In it, Fauchard describes the basic anatomy and function of the mouth, signs and symptoms of oral disease or pathology, operative methods for removing decay and restoring teeth, orthodontics, replacement of missing teeth, and even tooth transplantation. In preparing his book, Fauchard summarized all the then-available knowledge about dental anatomy, treatment of diseases, extraction and replacement of teeth, construction of dentures, and irregularities of teeth. In particular, he devoted an entire chapter of his book to orthodontics—the science of straightening teeth—the first major treatise on this topic.

Fauchard shared his knowledge and research with colleagues. This concept of sharing information helped to transform the dentist from a skilled artisan to a practitioner of medicine. The work of Fauchard led many others in England and Western Europe to publish their studies on topics such as care of teeth, their structures, and diseases. With this new interest in the practice of dentistry as a separate profession distinct from the medical profession, the foundation was laid for the practice of preventive and restorative dentistry as it is known today.

Dentistry in the United States

The emphasis on restorative dentistry found its way to the American colonies with the immigration of dentists in the 1700s, although the early focus was on removing diseased teeth and inserting artificial ones. Artificial teeth were made from a variety of different materials. The most common material for false teeth was animal bone or ivory, especially from elephants or hippopotami. People sometimes used human teeth, pulled from the dead or sold by poor people from their own mouths, as replacement teeth. These kinds of false teeth soon rotted, turning brown and rancid, and had to be replaced frequently. Rich people preferred teeth of silver, gold, mother of pearl, or agate. George Washington's teeth were not really made of wood, as is commonly thought; they were a combination of ivory, metal, and cow's teeth. Because the best materials used to make artificial teeth were so expensive, and because those who carved them were skilled artisans, false teeth were generally very expensive and, therefore, only the wealthy could afford them.

In America, dentistry as a profession and practice changed rapidly in a fairly short period. It began as a service provided by traveling practitioners. Many of these practitioners traversed a regular circuit from town to town, announcing their arrival in local newspapers. As the U.S. population increased and larger towns and cities sprang up, dentists stopped roaming from town to town and established a practice in one location. Early advertisements by surgeon-dentists (as they were then called) offered transplants of teeth, artificial teeth, and dentifrice (liquid, paste, or powder for cleaning teeth and gums).

Levi Spear Parmly (1790–1859), a New Orleans dentist, is credited as being the inventor of modern dental floss. He encouraged people to use silk thread to floss teeth as early as 1815. Sometimes dental practices merged with those of other occupations. A famous Revolutionary hero and silversmith, Paul Revere (1735–1818), also made artificial teeth and inserted them. Other practitioners began to specialize and to make improvements in existing techniques and tools. George Washington's dentist, John Greenwood (1760–1819), invented the first known "dental foot engine" in 1790, when he adapted his mother's foot-treadle spinning wheel to rotate a drill, thus freeing up his hands. Advancements in drill production and widespread use didn't occur until sometime later, after many others contributed to the production of the implements.

In the mid-1800s, a less expensive way to produce artificial teeth made them more available to the masses. Nelson Goodyear (1800–1860) discovered a process whereby tropical plant juices were hardened to produce a rubber that was then inserted into a patient's mouth to create a mold of his or her teeth. This enabled dentists to create a more precise base for introducing a porcelain artificial tooth; it was also more cost effective and often more comfortable for patients. The rubber was called *Vulcanite*, and it served as the foundation of dentures for many years, until about the 1940s, when acrylic replaced it.

Two other discoveries contributed a great deal to the progress of dentistry: anesthesia and radiography. Dr. Horace Wells (1815–48) of Connecticut first used anesthesia in dentistry in 1844, when he instructed a patient to inhale nitrous oxide before extracting a tooth. In 1864 the American Dental Association gave full credit to Horace Wells for the discovery of practical anesthesia. Unfortunately, deranged by self-experimentation with chloroform, he committed suicide in 1848. Surgeons and other medical practitioners now use anesthesia as a standard part of their practice. In 1895, in Germany, William Roentgen (1845–1923) discovered the X-ray. While this wasn't a U.S. discovery per se, the X-ray took hold in the United States and is another part of standard practice today. In fact, Dr. C. Edmund Kells (1856–1928), a New Orleans dentist, is credited as the first in the United States to use an X-ray machine in making radiographs of teeth. With radiographs, dentists could detect which teeth should be removed and which could be left safely in the mouth. Both discoveries eliminated a great deal of pain previously associated with dentistry.

Greene Vardiman Black (1836–1915), the first dean of Northwestern Dental School in Chicago, is best known as the person who fine-tuned dental techniques in the United States. In 1895 he standardized cavity preparation and amalgam manufacture. He also employed the sciences of biology and microbiology to study the mouth and teeth. In doing so, he identified a dense bacterial film that built up on teeth. He hypothesized that the buildup was responsible for infections resulting in dental caries (cavities) and oral disease. In fact, it wasn't until some time later, in about the 1960s, that scientific research confirmed his theory.

The twentieth century was a period of incredible progress in which preventive and cosmetic measures first appeared and established dental techniques were refined. Effective dental cement was developed and baked porcelain inlays came into use for filling large cavities. Metallic fillings were cast from a wax impression that matched the shape of the cavity perfectly. Hard as it may be to

imagine, regular tooth brushing did not become a habit of U.S. citizens until soldiers, who were trained to do so by the armed services
in World War II, brought the practice back with them from the war.

Twentieth Century to Today

Around the world, the major advances in the twentieth century that
ushered in the modern era of dentistry included anesthesia, the cre-
ation of new materials for dentures and artificial teeth, advancements in orthodontia (to be discussed in the following section), and
cosmetic dentistry. Advancements in anesthesia that began in the
mid-1800s with nitrous oxide or laughing gas and ether progressed
to less risky drugs, such as Novacaine in 1905 and its replacement
Lidocaine, discovered in 1943. These topical (meaning injected
into the tissue) agents are not very toxic and work almost instantly
to numb the tissue and provide fast pain relief. Materials improved
and became not only functional and durable, but also closely
approximated real oral structures. Fluoride was added to local water
supplies, which makes teeth more resistant to cavities; children are
often required to have fluoride treatments at each dental visit for
the same reason.

In the 1990s, after five patients of a dentist with AIDS became
infected with HIV, the Occupational Safety and Health Administration (OSHA) ruled that full protective garb (gloves, mask, glasses
or goggles, and coat) must be worn by dental personnel to protect
patients and themselves. Prior to this, gloves and masks were not
necessarily standard protocol in dentists' offices. Because of these
protective measures, there is now only a slim chance that anyone—
dentist or patient—would contract HIV from a dentist's office.

High technology and advanced scientific approaches character-
ize modern dentistry. One example is the treatment of receding

gums, which is caused by, among other things, genetics and heavy brushing with hard-bristled brushes. Grafts surgically replace receded gum tissue with regenerated tissues. The grafting procedure is meant to cover the exposed root surface, which can be incredibly painful, with a piece of gum tissue. This procedure provides protection for teeth, preventing them from having to be removed and replaced with a prosthetic. Another example is the use of various lasers, instead of the traditional drills, to fill cavities and cut gum tissue, tooth enamel, and bone. Lasers, including water lasers, are virtually painless and noiseless, making them a far less trauma-producing instrument.

The most recent developments in dentistry also include cosmetic advancements and the design of dental offices. People today want beautiful as well as healthy teeth, and they want to receive dental care in a relaxed and comfortable setting. Refinements in cosmetic dentistry include teeth whitening and porcelain veneers. Dental offices often have televisions, artwork, and fish tanks in the examination rooms—in addition to the latest technology. The goal is to make an experience that can be anxiety provoking and painful as pleasant as possible.

Orthodontia

Orthodontics, as a distinct science, developed during the 1880s and is the combined result of numerous practitioners' work. Pierre Fauchard was the first major authority to write about orthodontia in his book, as was described earlier. Another French dentist, Etienne Bourdet (1722–89), wrote the other seminal tome on orthodontics, *The Dentist's Art*. J. N. Farrar, the dentist who wrote *A Treatise on the Irregularities of the Teeth and Their Corrections*, designed brace appliances and was the first person to suggest applying mild force for periods of time to move teeth. Edward H. Angle (1855–1930) was the first person to identify the various kinds of malocclusions (uneven teeth). His classification system was a way for dentists to describe how crooked teeth are, what way teeth are pointing, and how teeth fit together. In 1901 he started the first school of orthodontics in St. Louis. The most recent developments in orthodontics include lighter materials and even removable braces for more comfortable and less-noticeable appliances.

Zia Chishti, a twenty-something graduate of both Columbia and Stanford universities, invented the newest technique in orthodontics—Invisalign braces. These are transparent, removable, and moldable braces. Instead of one pair of braces that are constantly adjusted, Invisaligns are a series of removable braces worn in succession. This type of orthodontia is a natural result of the public's desire for obtaining perfect teeth without substantially affecting their appearance with traditional metal braces.

Veterinary Dentistry

From ancient Chinese care to ancient Greek study, the earliest veterinary dentists tended to focus on examining and caring for horses' teeth. Because a horse's value was often based on the condition of its teeth—which were used to determine its age—it was important to keep the teeth in good repair. An early text by Aristotle in 333 B.C. called the *History of Animals* gave an account of periodontal disease in horses. Scholars of the Roman Empire wrote fairly extensively on the dentistry of various animals in addition to horses.

After the Middle Ages, which were also known as the Dark Ages for the lack of innovations, the science of veterinary dentistry began, once again, to advance. In 1762 the first veterinary dental school was founded in France. Various books published in the late

1800s and the early 1900s explored techniques in both equine and small-animal dentistry. In the 1930s Joseph Bodingbauer, a German veterinary dentist, was a pioneer in small animal dentistry. Widespread interest in veterinary dentistry didn't occur until the formation of the American Veterinary Dental Society (www.avds-online.org) in 1976. The American Veterinary Dental College (www.avdc.org) was formed in 1987 as more people became aware of the need to provide their pets with good oral care. Oral pathology, aging characteristics of teeth, and preventive measures are the focus of veterinary dentists today.

The First Formal Dental School

The first independent dental school in the United States and the first formal school in the world—the Baltimore College of Dental Surgery—opened in 1840. Before that time dentists underwent an apprenticeship to learn their craft, and it was customary for anyone, with or without formal education, to become a dentist by serving five years of apprenticeship. However, the kind of training these fledgling dentists received depended entirely on the knowledge and skill of the dentist with whom they were associated. In some instances, training was of acceptable quality; in others, it was not.

Formal training at the Baltimore College of Dental Surgery consisted of two full courses of lectures for four months, in addition to performing dental operations and preparing and setting artificial teeth. Students were also required to write a thesis on some aspect of dentistry. If the faculty members found the student candidates competent after examination, they were then awarded the degree of Doctor of Dental Surgery, the first use of the now-familiar D.D.S.

From this first dental school, a system of accredited dental schools, each associated with a college or university, has evolved.

There are currently more than sixty such programs that offer modern dental health education for dentists in the United States and Canada, some of which offer the Doctor of Medical Dentistry (D.M.D.) degree. (See Appendix A for a list of the schools and their websites.)

There is no difference between the two dentistry degrees, the D.D.S. and the D.M.D. The same education is required to achieve both degrees; it is up to the individual college or university to determine what degree is awarded. The American Dental Association's Commission on Dental Accreditation sets the same curriculum requirements for both degrees, and state licensing boards accept either degree as equivalent.

For many years dentists worked alone, performing nearly all of the functions needed in the office; gradually the concept of an organized dental team developed. Today's dental practices include not only the services of the dentist but also those of the dental hygienist, dental assistant, and laboratory technician. The following sections describe, in brief, the history of the various members of the dental support team.

History of Dental Hygiene

Dental hygiene, as a separate function, is only about one hundred years old. Prior to the early 1900s, the main function of dentists was to address any dental problems as they arose, usually through the extraction and replacement of teeth. There is evidence, however, of sporadic efforts to promote oral hygiene and cleanliness of the teeth as early as the middle to late 1800s, but the idea never really caught on.

Dr. Alfred Fones (1869–1938) of Bridgeport, Connecticut, is widely considered to be the "father of dental hygiene." Fones believed that teaching basic oral hygiene measures could prevent many problems from occurring in the first place. Unfortunately, educating patients about oral hygiene was very time-consuming so, in 1906, Fones trained his office assistant, Mrs. Irene Newman, in both oral cleaning and in providing dental health education. From this, the idea of employing someone whose sole job was to teach preventive measures took hold and spread across the United States.

In 1913, through Dr. Fones's efforts, the city of Bridgeport appropriated five thousand dollars to start an educational program teaching dental hygiene in the city schools. The Fones School of Dental Hygiene at the University of Bridgeport (www.bridge port.edu), the first dental hygiene school in the world, was located next to Dr. Fones's office; thirty-four young women entered the program at its onset. The faculty members were dentists from the area and instructors for dental and medical schools.

From this first class (which included schoolteachers, nurses, and dental assistants), ten hygienists were employed by the city of Bridgeport. A health-education program was started in which the new dental hygienists presented classroom talks and training. Programs for parents were sponsored. The hygienists performed cleaning functions for the schoolchildren and kept dental records for them, too. In collecting the data, these hygienists developed the first dental public health program.

The first courses at the Fones School were so successful that three more schools were started—two in New York and one in Massachusetts. The first of these new schools, the New York School of Dental Hygiene, was started in 1916 by Dr. Louise Ball; it is now a department of the College of Dental Surgery of Columbia University. The second school was started at the Eastman Dental Dispensary in Rochester, New York, and the third at the Forsyth Dental Dispensary for Children in Boston, Massachusetts. Only fourteen more schools were started between 1913 and 1946; however, since 1946 the number has increased rapidly. Currently there are approximately two hundred training programs to meet the demand for the services of dental hygienists and nearly 120,000 working in the field.

Licensure and registration of dental hygienists and the organization of associations soon followed the establishment of the schools. The American Dental Hygienists' Association (ADHA) was formed in 1923 to develop communication and mutual cooperation among dental hygienists (www.adha.org). In 1946 a committee from the American Dental Association (www.ada.org) set requirements for existing schools of dental hygiene so that each school offered similar basic programs. After meeting these basic requirements, each school may vary its programs as needed. By 1951 dental hygienists were licensed in all states. At first, dental hygienists were almost exclusively women; the first man received his license in the late 1950s in Oregon.

As education and training have advanced, the duties of the hygienist have changed. In all states, the hygienist is licensed to perform functions related to cleaning and education, but, in some states, the hygienist can perform expanded functions related to placement of fillings and administration of anesthesia.

History of Dental Assisting

The man who pioneered the use of dental X-rays, Dr. C. Edmund Kells (1856–1930), was the first to hire a woman as an assistant. Men had been working as assistants, often as apprentices, in 1885, and this was a daring change. At that time, a woman did not come alone to a dental office for treatment; her husband or a companion accompanied her. After Dr. Kells's practice prospered, other dentists began to hire female assistants. The sign "Lady in Attendance" was placed in the windows of many dental offices, and women felt more comfortable entering these offices alone. Slowly, more and more women were hired.

Although many assistants were trained on the job, formal training programs were gradually established. In the 1940s the Education Committee of the American Dental Assistants Association (www.dentalassistant.org) outlined the first basic course of study. The plan provided for a 104-hour course of study on subjects pertaining to dental procedures. In 1954 the University of North Carolina Dental School began a special correspondence school for dental assistants. By that time the demand for assistants exceeded the supply, and more trained assistants were needed.

As more and more assistants were employed, their responsibilities increased. Although their duties include office management and clerical work, today many assistants work directly with patients and alongside dentists. The assistants participate in technical procedures that do not directly require the professional knowledge and judgment of the dentist and improve the dentist's productivity and ability to provide more efficient dental care.

History of Dental Laboratory Technology

Dental laboratory technicians are involved in the manufacturing of corrective devices and replacements for natural teeth. Some of the people who could be called the earliest laboratory technicians were silversmiths and goldsmiths who formed artificial teeth as a sideline to their work of sculpture, jewelry making, and other crafts. These people worked either independently for a client or with a dentist to help solve a client's problem with artificial teeth or dentures. As noted previously, Paul Revere was of this type; as such, he may be considered an early dental technician.

In 1883 Dr. W. H. Stowe, a Boston dentist, became the first to specialize in dental technology. Dr. Stowe, who was known for his work crafting artificial teeth, found that he had little time for his own dental practice after accepting prosthetic work from other dentists. By 1887 the laboratory services he provided had become so successful that he left his practice for good and concentrated on his prosthetic skills. By the beginning of the twentieth century, many laboratories had been established. In 1920 there were nearly two thousand laboratories in the United States. Today there are about ninety-five hundred in operation.

As in dentistry, a pattern of educating technicians from apprenticeship through training programs was initially developed, and eventually formal educational programs were formed. Formal education in dental technology has grown from three accredited two-year programs in 1961 to more than thirty programs today. Currently, dental laboratory technicians receive formal education in all pertinent subjects through precise and scientific training.

Now that you know a little bit about the history of dentistry and the various dental team members, the following chapter takes a closer look inside today's dentist's office.

2

WORKING AS A DENTIST

THE DENTIST IS the person with the greatest responsibility and the one usually in charge of the dental practice. It is also the position that enjoys the most financial compensation. Dentists today have a variety of exciting areas in which to work and specialize. They use the latest scientific advancements and research to provide care. Best of all, they can work just about anywhere from Small Town, U.S.A., to the largest metropolitan areas.

Today's dental practices are high-tech, pleasant places to work. Patients have less fear of visiting dentists because of the established culture in the United States of preventive dentistry, which means fewer dental problems and painful treatment procedures. People understand that regular dental care is an important part of maintaining good health. Consequently, they come to the dentist's office regularly.

This chapter describes the work of the dentist in detail. From general practice to areas of specialty, you'll learn what the work is like for this important member of the health care team. Perhaps when you've finished reading this chapter, you'll have found your career calling, so read on.

What a Dentist Does

Dentists diagnose, prevent, and treat problems with teeth or mouth tissue. They remove decay, fill cavities, examine X-rays, place protective plastic sealants on children's teeth, straighten teeth, and repair fractured teeth. They also perform corrective surgery on gums and supporting bones to treat gum diseases. Dentists extract teeth and make models and measurements for dentures to replace them using a variety of equipment, including drills, and instruments such as mouth mirrors, probes, forceps, brushes, and scalpels. They provide instruction on diet, brushing, flossing, the use of fluoride, and other aspects of dental care. They also administer anesthetics and write prescriptions for antibiotics and other medications.

The dentist has several objectives to accomplish during the first interview with the patient. He or she should have a good idea of the complete dental and partial medical history of the patient based on information gathered from the patient's chart. The focus of the history is on previous treatment of dental problems, any major health concerns, and specific medications the patient is taking, in addition to other topics. The dentist also evaluates the patient's nutritional health and emotional stability during the visit from first introduction and throughout the exam. After the oral examination, the dentist records the findings, including a diagnosis of the problem, if there is one, and treatment provided and/or required. The goals of the total treatment plan are to eliminate any disease and restore the patient's mouth to its normal function, counsel the patient in self-care procedures, and give follow-up professional care to prevent recurrence of the disease.

Dentists typically receive assistance in their practice from dental hygienists, dental assistants, and dental laboratory technicians. In particular, the dental lab tech has taken over many of the tasks that were once in the domain of the dentist. Having the hygienist handle additional treatment procedures is more economically feasible, as the dentist is then free to provide the more complicated procedures that are needed for the patient. These members of the dental support staff are discussed in detail in the following chapter.

The general practitioner with a dental degree can and does perform many or all parts of the duties of more specialized dentists in the everyday office routine. General practitioners also know when a specialist must be consulted—when a patient's condition requires additional treatment beyond the scope of the practitioner. Dental care practitioners must have this spirit of cooperation to ensure the best possible treatment for patients.

Special Patients

Dentists spend more time and use different skills when working with special needs patients. Mentally disabled patients often require extensive reassurance and a calm approach using simple, non-threatening language to describe the procedures being done to them. Dentists seeing patients in hospitals for long-term stays may be the first to observe the beginning of a problem in the mouth of the hospitalized patient. In working with the homebound patient, the dentist will often have to bring special equipment with him or her. In caring for the geriatric (elderly) patient, the dentist must learn to recognize the changes in tissues, skin, and muscles that can affect the condition of the aging mouth; the dentist must pay particular attention to oral tissues because of the frequent occurrence of oral cancer in older populations.

Emergency Care

From time to time, the dentist must handle emergencies that can occur in the office or other practice setting. Types of emergencies that can occur include prolonged bleeding caused by disease or blood thinning medication, difficulty breathing, shock, heart failure, seizures, or fainting. Dentists must be kept up to date on the first aid procedures for each of these conditions. Knowing the technique for cardiopulmonary resuscitation and artificial respiration is invaluable in a crisis situation. Some states require training for resuscitation to get licensure.

It is not often that a dentist will need to provide emergency care in the form of first aid measures, but the individual trained in a health care profession must be able to react correctly if such a need arises. The first step is, of course, to understand the patient's needs well enough so that emergencies can be prevented. If an adequate history has been taken, the dentist will be aware of any special physical conditions that could require first aid. The dentist will also have information concerning allergies or drug reactions, or any disease for which the patient is under the care of a physician and the prescribed type of treatment.

Job Outlook

According to the U.S. Bureau of Labor Statistics, employment of dentists is expected to grow more slowly than the average for all occupations through 2012. While employment growth will provide some job opportunities, most jobs will result from the need to replace the large number of dentists projected to retire. For greater stability, new dentists can join the practice of an older dentist and eventually take over the practice when the senior dentist retires. Job prospects in general should be good if the number of dental school graduates does not grow significantly, thus keeping the supply of newly qualified dentists near current levels.

Demand for dental care should grow substantially through 2012. As members of the baby-boom generation advance into middle age, a large number will need maintenance on complicated dental work such as bridges. In addition, today elderly people are more likely to retain their teeth than their predecessors, so they will require much more care than in the past. The younger generation will continue to need preventive checkups despite treatments such as fluoridation of the water supply, which decreases the incidence of tooth decay.

However, the employment of dentists is not expected to grow as rapidly as the demand for dental services. As their practices expand, dentists are likely to hire more dental hygienists and dental assistants to handle routine services they now perform themselves.

Salaries for Dentists

According to the Bureau of Labor Statistics, the median annual earnings of salaried dentists are $123,210. Earnings vary according to number of years in practice, location, hours worked, and specialty. Dentists in the early years of their practice often earn less, and they have school loans to pay off and the extra expense of setting up a new office. Those established in careers tend to earn more.

A relatively large proportion of dentists are self-employed. In general, self-employed dentists in private practice tend to earn more than salaried dentists. Like other business owners, these dentists must provide their own health insurance, life insurance, and retirement benefits; they also must pay salaries to dental assistants, hygienists, and other staff members.

Areas of Specialty

Although most dentists are general practitioners and handle a variety of dental needs, other dentists practice in any of nine specialty areas. Orthodontists, the largest group of specialists, straighten teeth by applying pressure to the teeth with braces or retainers. The next largest group, oral and maxillofacial surgeons, operates on the mouth and jaws. The remainder may specialize as pediatric dentists (focusing on dentistry for children); periodontists (treating gums and bone supporting the teeth); prosthodontists (replacing missing teeth with permanent fixtures such as crowns and bridges or with removable fixtures such as dentures); endodontists (performing root canal therapy); public-health dentists (promoting good dental health and preventing dental diseases within the community); oral pathologists (studying oral diseases); or oral and maxillofacial radiologists (diagnosing diseases in the head and neck through the use of imaging technologies). Most, if not all, of these specialties require additional, usually advanced education to gain entry into the field. As a result, they also receive greater compensation than the dentist in general practice. (See the ADA website for more information on the specialties and accredited educational programs at www.ada.org.) The following sections touch on the areas of specialty in dentistry.

Orthodontics

All orthodontists are, first of all, dentists, but only about 6 percent of dentists are orthodontists. This branch of dentistry is concerned with correcting irregularities of teeth to provide normal occlusion (alignment of teeth in the mouth), plus a pleasing appearance. Correction of these irregularities improves appearance, chewing ability, and speech habits and often lessens pain.

The way in which orthodontists reposition teeth is a very time-consuming process. First, orthodontists make models or casts of the patient's mouth to show how the irregular teeth can be corrected. Correction is typically in the form of applying fixed appliances or braces to the teeth in the patient's mouth. Treatment can last from two to four years, during which time the patient initially makes weekly visits, then monthly appointments. The braces, which are adjusted by the orthodontist, move the teeth gradually into a better arrangement. The final results offer correct position of teeth, normal use of the muscles of the mouth, and better general health.

Orthodontics is a team effort. Orthodontists typically work in private offices with orthodontic chair-side assistants, orthodontic office administrators, and sometimes with orthodontist partners. The work is fairly regular because treatments go on for such long periods. The downside of this delay is that the orthodontist often has to offer patients reassurance and encouragement to keep their spirits up about the final product. In addition to being expert diagnosticians, good orthodontists must also have a great deal of patience because they must deal with many different kinds of people, from staff to patients and their parents. Most orthodontic patients are children, but many adults concerned with their physical appearance also see orthodontists.

Orthodontists must complete additional education and training beyond graduation from a dental program. Admission to orthodontic postgraduate programs is extremely competitive and selective. As in medicine, the educational requirements are demanding. First, an orthodontist must complete college. Then, students must complete a three- to four-year graduate program at a dental school in a university or other institution accredited by the American Dental Association. Finally, students must receive at least two or three years of advanced specialty education in an accredited orthodontic residency program. These rigorous programs include advanced education in biomedical, behavioral, and basic sciences. During the residency, the orthodontist learns the complex skills required to both manage tooth movement (orthodontics) and guide facial development (dentofacial orthopedics).

Oral and Maxillofacial Surgery

Oral and maxillofacial surgeons perform a range of surgical operations. Their work encompasses the diagnosis, surgery, and related management of diseases, injuries, and defects of both the functional and aesthetic aspects of the mouth. This includes preventive, reconstructive, or emergency care for the teeth, mouth, jaws, and facial structures. Oral surgeons repair defects of the mouth, either those that appear at birth or those caused by an accident. They realign mouth structures, such as the upper jaw (maxilla) or the lower jaw (mandible), through breaking bone and wiring it into the proper position. They remove tumors and teeth. While they usually don't administer the anesthesia required to sedate someone during surgery, oral surgeons must have a complete knowledge of the use of anesthesia and its effects.

In this part of dentistry, people must be on call for emergencies. The oral surgeon is often affiliated with a university or hospital or both. Many patients may have been in accidents or have problems that require immediate attention. Unfortunately, these problems do not always occur during regular office hours.

Those considering this dental specialty must be prepared to go on for several more years of graduate study after receiving their degrees in general dentistry. This usually means at least four years of hospital-based surgical residency training that includes rotations in the general surgical service working alongside other physician surgeons. Those hoping to be oral surgeons must also pass several examinations: oral and written tests, plus a clinical test in which the actual diagnosis and treatment of patients are required. Finally, oral surgeons must achieve certification by the American Board of Oral and Maxillofacial Surgery (www.aboms.org), the certifying board for the specialty of oral and maxillofacial surgery in the United States.

Pediatric Dentistry

Pediatric dentists take care of children and teach them how to care for their teeth. Pediatric dentists must understand the processes of how the child's mouth develops. Because the primary (baby) set of teeth is important to the correct development of the permanent teeth, they must be cared for and treated when problems arise. In fact, pediatric dentistry starts before babies have teeth, with dentists teaching parents or pregnant women never to put babies to bed with a bottle of juice or milk. Limiting such sugar-filled drinks ensures that teeth, when they do come in, are more likely to be healthy.

Children taught the importance of caring for their teeth are more likely to become adults that care for their teeth. Good oral hygiene habits can be instilled early, and this is an important part of the pediatric dentist's job. A background strong in child psychology will benefit the dentist practicing in this area in teaching these skills and helping children overcome fears of the dental office or instruments. Much patience and understanding is required from those planning a career in pediatric dentistry.

In a pediatric practice, the dentist should be aware of what type of activity or explanation appeals to each age group. For example, a three-year-old child who may be making a first visit to the office usually has a friendly attitude and a desire to talk, making it difficult to have the child remain quiet long enough to perform a satisfactory examination. The dentist can use a positive, friendly approach and simple language with little explanation. Sometimes a prop, such as a puppet, can be useful. Four- and five-year-old children can be quite cooperative and begin to understand the process and importance of cleaning teeth. Often, a child this age can be so eager to please and so impressed with the importance of tooth brushing that he or she will not go to bed without brushing. A six-year-old child just entering school may be having to move from close family ties for the first time and may resent any additional intrusion. If too much stress is placed on a child whose behavior is already a problem, the dental experience may not be a happy one. In some instances, it is best to postpone treatment. Until the age of twelve, when the child patient is almost an adult, the growing-up process may offer problems not related to the dental office but may cause the child to resent treatment. Special patience and understanding are required to meet not only children's dental needs but also their emotional needs. Understanding children's capabilities and habits will help the dentist work successfully.

Advanced education in pediatric dentistry is typically two years of additional study. Programs emphasize various phases of pediatric dentistry including trauma, preventive dentistry, restorative dentistry, endodontics, periodontics, oral surgery, orthodontics, and hospital dentistry. Students learn various treatments for pain control and behavioral management, such as sedation, analgesia, and general anesthesia. Upon completion, pediatric dentists can provide comprehensive oral health care for the well child, the medically compromised, and children with special needs. Graduates are either awarded a master's degree or a certificate in pediatric dentistry.

Periodontics

The supporting tissues of the teeth are called gums or, scientifically, the gingiva of the mouth. If this gingiva is destroyed, teeth are lost. Poor occlusion, food impaction, incorrect or inadequate restoration of teeth, irritants of several types, or a disease that affects other parts of the body as well as teeth can all cause destruction of the gingiva. As the gingiva becomes infected, bacteria can enter and destroy tissue. Specialists in periodontics must diagnose and stop this destructive process.

Periodontists work almost entirely with adult patients because diseases of the gingiva typically take time to develop. The cause of the loss of gingiva can be complex, so that knowledge of the disease process is required. If the patient has a disease that affects other parts of the body, the periodontist must work with a laboratory and other means of diagnosis to determine the exact cause and cure. Surgery is often performed in which part of the infected gingiva is removed. Preventive treatment is usually the most effective method of control. Periodontists must perform thorough cleaning of a patient's teeth and gums and instruct the patient in correct cleaning processes to prevent recurrence of the disease.

Prosthodontics

Prosthodontists are concerned with the replacement of teeth that have been lost because of disease or accidents. Replacement can be of a single tooth or all of the teeth in the mouth. A prosthodontist can also reconstruct parts of the jaws with artificial substitutes.

Dentists may practice general dentistry along with performing prosthodontic treatment. However, patients experiencing problems with their replacement teeth may consult a prosthodontic specialist to correct the problem. The specialist must be skilled in all the new processes of restoration so that the replacement teeth not only fit properly but also enhance the patient's appearance. Dental laboratory technicians assist prosthodontists in constructing the correct replacements for teeth.

Patients who consult prosthodontists may have teeth so badly deformed or diseased that the teeth may all have to be extracted. The specialist must then reconstruct the entire mouth of the patient with complete dentures or with implants, providing teeth that fit and perform correctly and give a pleasing appearance. Much skill, time, and effort are required to achieve this finished effect.

A prosthodontist's education includes several years of postgraduate training in complicated techniques and treatments, including the following:

Dental implants
Crowns and bridges
Denture fabrication and therapy
Fixed and removable partial dentures
Temporomandibular disorders (TMD/TMJ)
Cosmetic dentistry
Facial replacements
Total mouth rehabilitation
Dental trauma related to accidents and cancer treatment

Endodontics

This fairly new specialty of dentistry deals with the treatment of the pulp of a tooth, which can mean the difference between saving and extracting a tooth. The procedure involves careful, sterile treatment of the roots of the teeth. Each tooth has one or more roots at its base, and each root has one or more canals in its center.

Within each canal is a small opening so that the blood vessels and nerves of the pulp can connect with similar structures in the bone surrounding the root end. Any damage to this system will eventually result in the destruction and loss of the tooth.

If the pulp tissue is injured (by an accident or blow to the teeth) or decay has reached the tissue, the pulp tissue must be removed and the area filled with a sterile material. During treatment, which often involves from one to three visits, the endodontist removes the diseased pulp and then cleans and seals the pulp chamber and root canal. First, an opening is made through the crown of the tooth and into the pulp chamber (this is the root canal). The pulp is then removed and the root canal is cleaned and shaped to a form that can be filled. Medications may be added to the root canal to kill germs and prevent infection. A temporary filling will be placed in the crown opening to protect the tooth between dental visits, or the endodontist may leave the tooth open for a few days to drain. Finally, the pulp chamber and root canals are filled and sealed and a gold or porcelain crown is placed over the tooth. As long as the root of a treated tooth is nourished by the tissues around it, the tooth should remain healthy and not cause any further problems.

The endodontist must possess certain skills to be good at this job. Manual dexterity is required to perform these sensitive procedures. The endodontist must have knowledge of the biology of the pulp as well as the anatomy of the teeth and jaws. This specialist must also learn a great deal about both oral pathology (study of diseases) and bacteriology (study of microscopic organisms that can cause diseases).

Dental Public Health

A career in public health dentistry offers a chance to serve a community rather than an individual patient. The responsibility of this career is preventive dentistry on a large scale and not in a clinical setting. People in public health service are concerned with controlling dental diseases, educating the public, and promoting dental health through organized efforts. They work with community leaders to develop, implement, and support practices that will promote oral health, eliminate oral health disparities, and improve the quality of life of the community members.

There are also many opportunities for research in public health dentistry. Researchers may study the effects of fluoridation on schoolchildren or methods to decrease tooth decay. The results of the research are often applied in organized community projects. Public health dentists may use the newest research tools such as electron microscopes to conduct their studies. In many instances, they work in federal government laboratories, and the government will distribute the results of their research and study.

Finally, some public health dentists choose to work in colleges and universities and for the government. Academic opportunities include both research and teaching. Government jobs can be found within organizations such as the Department of Health and Human Services (www.hhs.gov).

Oral Pathology

Oral pathology is the specialty of dentistry and pathology that deals with the nature, identification, and management of diseases affecting the oral and maxillofacial regions. It is a science that investigates the causes, effects, and treatment of these diseases. Areas of study range from oral cancer to problems with smell and taste to bone deformities resulting in facial pain.

Although oral pathologists focus on diseases of the mouth, they must also have a thorough understanding of the pathophysiology of the entire human body. For example, oral pathologists study tumors of the mouth. Treatment for many types of tumors is radiation. The oral pathologist must be aware of the effects of radiation not only on the mouth and the tumor but also on the rest of the body and its cells.

Oral pathologists work primarily in a laboratory, although they may also have office practices. They may teach or do research for a college or for a branch of the military services. People who choose this part of dentistry must be interested in extensive research and use of such laboratory procedures as clinical, microscopic, radiographic, and biochemical examinations.

Oral and Maxillofacial Radiology

Oral and maxillofacial radiology is the specialty of dentistry concerned with the use of imaging and associated technology for diagnosis and treatment of diseases affecting the mouth, jaws, and face. An understanding of the basic principles and applications of all diagnostic imaging methods used in dentistry and other health care professions is fundamental to the discipline. The science of oral and maxillofacial radiology is based on principles of physics, chemistry, and biology.

The work of these radiologists involves working with and sometimes even helping create new and cutting edge technologies. Oral and maxillofacial radiologists interpret traditional radiographs or X-rays, such as those made in dental offices, as well as digital imagery, conventional and computed tomography (CT), magnetic resonance imaging (MRI), and nuclear medicine. Radiologists help general practice dentists understand what they're seeing on a variety of different styles of imagery.

Education to become a radiologist includes teaching dental students about the principles and applications of ionizing radiation in the diagnosis of disease. This includes ensuring that the students have an appreciation for radiation physics, the biologic hazards that result from using ionizing radiation, as well as the general use of radiographs to identify both normal anatomy and pathologic conditions. Typical courses include preclinical laboratory exercises to develop practical skills in radiographic procedures as well as self-instruction materials that cover normal radiographic anatomy to serve as the foundation for future radiographic interpretation and patient care. Basics of interpretation and principles of advanced imaging methods, such as CT, MRI, and functional studies, are also taught in these courses. Educational material is designed to prepare the advanced practitioner in radiologic management of patients with complex diagnostic problems.

3

Assistive Personnel

As you know, a dentist is not the only person who repairs teeth. A dentist's office is filled with a variety of individuals who make up the dental team and, while they may perform many diverse tasks, they typically have a few things in common. Those likely to have a rewarding career in dentistry typically possess intelligence, ambition, and social awareness along with scientific curiosity.

The range of opportunities for dental hygienists, dental assistants, and laboratory technicians is increasing as their responsibilities expand. For example, in addition to working in a dentist's office or in a laboratory, there are numerous other fascinating fields of service. In this chapter, you'll read about the numerous job opportunities available for the other vital members of the dental care team as well as what the jobs entail and salaries for each position, starting with the dental hygienist.

Dental Hygienists

As defined by the American Dental Hygienists' Association (www
.adha.org), dental hygiene is the health profession that "in cooperation with the dental profession, provides services to promote opti-
mal oral health care for the public." The work of dental hygienists
→ is becoming increasingly more specialized and, in some instances,
more independent. State law regulates the functions performed by
dental hygienists, so they may vary slightly from state to state. For
the most part, however, hygienists perform the following tasks that
help the dentist provide complete dental care:

- Collect information about the patient for a medical and
  dental history
- Remove accumulated material from teeth
- Take and process X-rays
- Analyze patient's diet and counsel about nutrition
- Instruct patient in correct brushing and cleaning habits
- Apply cavity-preventive agents such as sealants and fluoride
- Make impressions of patient's teeth for study models used to
  evaluate treatment needs
- Design and consult with dental health programs in schools
  and communities

Nearly all dental hygienists use hand and rotary instruments and
ultrasonics to clean and polish teeth, X-ray machines to take dental pictures, syringes with needles to administer local anesthetics,
and models of teeth to explain oral hygiene. Although hygienists
may not diagnose diseases, they can prepare clinical and laboratory
diagnostic tests for the dentist to interpret.

Some states have even expanded the duties of the hygienist under general supervision to include placing and removing defective restorations and periodontal dressings, polishing and recontouring defective restorations, administering local anesthesia, removing sutures, and placing and carving some types of restorations. The term *general supervision* has been interpreted to mean supervision of dental procedures based on the authorization given by a licensed dentist, but not requiring the physical presence of the supervising dentist during the performance of some procedures. Supervision must meet standards set by state laws. A general supervision requirement may be met, for example, when the dentist writes the prescription for a cleaning for a patient or does the examination to diagnose a cleaning. Similarly, the treatment facility in which a hygienist works may be under the jurisdiction and control of a supervising licensed dentist.

The type of patient a hygienist sees varies depending on the type of practice. In a general practice setting, the hygienist works with patients of all ages and types of conditions. The hygienist learns to cope with children who come for their first appointments, with people of every age who have neglected care of their teeth, and with elderly patients in nursing homes and hospitals, where the hygienist is often the primary provider of dental care. In an office in which special oral conditions are treated, the hygienist must acquire additional knowledge about these conditions. For example, if the dentist is a pediatric dentist, the hygienist should have training in child psychology to be able to teach children about the care of their teeth, to give them nutritional advice, and to make their experience in a dental office as pleasant as possible. In orthodontic practice, hygienists see the patients for long periods, as the corrective movement of teeth is a gradual process. Hygienists prepare full-mouth X-rays, make impressions for study casts, and perform cleaning and fluoride treatments. The hygienist also gives complete instructions about home care and eating habits when correctional appliances are worn. The treatment of all patients includes instructing them about care of their teeth and gums.

The dental hygienist, working in any setting, is often the first person to see a patient and frequently is the one who remains in closest contact with the patient in follow-up care and treatment. The hygienist's concern for preventing dental disease is evident in the way the hygienist instructs patients. Cleaning the teeth may be the most valuable of all tasks, as the hygienist can instruct while the cleaning takes place.

Individualized instruction becomes very important in the first and follow-up visits. The hygienist must emphasize, in many ways depending on the age and experience of the patient, the importance of brushing and cleaning the teeth. The hygienist can demonstrate correct brushing and flossing techniques, using methods suitable for each age group. In dealing with children, the hygienist must be careful to explain the activity in terms the child can understand. Special problems that arise when working with adolescents, such as removing material from beneath braces or other oral devices, must be solved. For older adults, self-care may focus on properly cleaning prosthetic devices.

Teaching Program

With patients of any age, an effective teaching program provides both detailed information and principles to guide and motivate the patient. With the hygienist's concern and professional enthusiasm, patients can be motivated to cooperate. Several basic steps can be used:

1. **Demonstration.** The patient should be taught how to hold the brush and the correct methods of brushing and flossing.
2. **Evaluation.** A disclosing tablet that stains the teeth in areas where cleaning is incomplete can be used to show the patient how well he or she has brushed.
3. **Practice.** During the second or third visit, the patient should be able to show how well brushing has been practiced at home.
4. **Results.** The patient's progress should be recorded, and the hygienist should point out the improvement, or lack of it, and discuss in an encouraging manner how to solve any problems.

Other Procedures

Oral surgery procedures require the use of anesthesia, and hygienists, because of their formal education and training, can be a part of this health care delivery system. The hygienist can be involved in various phases of anesthesia administration, from the preparation of the drug for the dentist to the actual administration of the drug, if permitted by state law. It is often the hygienist's responsibility to monitor the patient for the duration of the drug's effect so that the drug's actions, including side effects, will be known. The hygienist can prepare the patient for the surgical procedure and for follow-up care when nutritional intake is limited by the oral surgery procedure.

In addition to responsibility during oral surgery procedures, the hygienist can be the clinician or advisor before, during, and after treatment of periodontal (gum) disease by a periodontist. The hygienist can also aid the orthodontist by teaching patients how to care for teeth while braces are worn. To be helpful in more detailed treatment, the hygienist must have a reasonable working knowledge of malocclusion (a problem with the way teeth come together), its cause, and treatment.

Work Settings and Hours

Some people with a Master of Public Health (M.P.H.) degree, and some dental hygienists without the degree, choose to work in public health. Each state has a department of public health, and many employ dental hygienists for community health education and administrative work. This work can be as varied as lecturing on fluoridation of water, preparing pamphlets and films for distribution in schools, and conducting training sessions for elementary-school teachers. Hygienists may be employed by a school system to both work directly with schoolchildren and train those who do.

There are a variety of opportunities for dental hygienists to work with the disabled. Some hygienists work in hospitals as part of a dental program. Others work with disabled patients in hospitals and other institutions. In these situations, the hygienist serves the disabled for whom special cleaning aids might be devised, for example, specially bent or longer handles on toothbrushes or electric toothbrushes mounted on brackets. For mentally disabled persons, the hygienist must employ other methods to encourage and reinforce these patients in the care of their teeth.

With nearly two hundred schools offering training programs for dental hygienists, there is a need for teachers. Teaching duties depend on the specialty of the hygienist and usually include supervision of students as they learn to work with patients in actual clinical settings. Benefits for those who teach include having summers off and a more flexible schedule.

Chances to work abroad are also available for the dental hygienist. In some European countries, dental hygiene as a distinct profession is fairly new. Dental hygienists in Great Britain, however, have been working independently since 1957. In New Zealand, dental nurses provide all dental care for children up to age twelve. Duties of the profession can change from country to country, so a study of each one and its language should be part of any decision to work abroad. Your school can usually help you make such a decision and may even have study abroad programs that can give you a feel for a particular country.

From the descriptions of careers in dental hygiene, you can see that hours and working conditions do not always ensure a forty-hour workweek; indeed, flexible scheduling is a distinctive feature of this job. Hours can be spent in a nine-to-five routine, perhaps four and a half weekdays, plus a half-day on Saturdays. Traveling from one school to another can be part of the schedule for a school employee. Hours in the classroom and preparing for lectures can add up to more than a forty-hour week for an educator.

Dental hygiene is a career that can be adjusted to many lifestyles. Hygienists can work part-time, which is especially good for those with a young family. They can also share a job with another hygienist, which allows both workers to keep up their clinical skills. Many hygienists work as independent contractors, in a business agreement between the hygienist and dentist. There are many options in this career.

Employment Outlook

The role of the dental hygienist has moved from focusing solely on preventive care to also providing a variety of treatments and interventions. The responsibility of the dental hygienist has become one in which more knowledge and training have led to increased duties and additional functions. As some form of dental disease or problem affects approximately 90 percent of the U.S. population, the need for preventive dentistry and treatment is extensive, and services of the dental hygienist are very much in demand.

Dental hygienists hold about 150,000 jobs throughout the United States and Canada. Because it is common in this field for hygienists to hold multiple jobs, the number of jobs greatly exceeds the number of hygienists. More than half of all dental hygienists work part-time—fewer than thirty-five hours a week—and almost all work in private dental offices. The remainder are employed by public health agencies, hospitals, school systems, industrial plants, dental hygiene schools, research centers, and state and federal government agencies. Some work overseas and on military bases.

According to the U.S. Bureau of Labor Statistics (www.bls.gov), employment of dental hygienists is expected to grow much faster than the average for all occupations through the year 2012, in response to increasing demand for dental care and the greater substitution of hygienists for services previously performed by dentists. Job prospects are expected to remain very good, unless the number of dental hygienist program graduates grows much faster than during the last decade, resulting in a much larger pool of qualified applicants. Demand will be stimulated by population growth and greater retention of natural teeth by the larger number of middle-aged and elderly people. Also, dentists are likely to employ more hygienists for several reasons. As dentists' workloads increase, they are expected to hire more hygienists to perform preventive dental care such as cleaning, so they may devote their own time to more profitable procedures. Older dentists, who are less likely to employ dental hygienists, will leave and be replaced by recent graduates, who are more likely to do so.

Salaries for Dental Hygienists

Of all the assistive personnel, dental hygienists generally command the highest salaries. Geographic location, employment setting, education, and experience affect earnings of dental hygienists. Dental hygienists working in private dental offices may be paid on an hourly, daily, salary, or commission basis. According to government statistics, the median hourly earnings of dental hygienists were $26.59 in 2002. The middle 50 percent earned between $21.96 and $32.48 an hour. The lowest 10 percent earned less than $17.34, and the highest 10 percent earned more than $39.24 an hour. In terms of yearly salary, this means that the middle 50 percent earned between $45,677 and $67,559 per year. The lowest 10 percent earned less than $36,068 and the highest 10 percent earned more than $81,800.

Benefits vary substantially by practice setting and are often contingent upon full-time employment. Dental hygienists who work for school systems, public health agencies, the federal government, or state agencies usually have substantial benefits. Dental hygienists who work overseas may also be provided with additional perks such as free transportation, housing allowances, and longer paid vacations.

Dental Assistants

Dental assistants perform a variety of patient care, office, and laboratory duties. They work alongside dentists as they examine and treat patients. According to the American Dental Assistants Association (www.dentalassistant.org), dental assistants "assist with the direct care of patients under the supervision of a dentist." This valuable assistance may take the following forms:

- Helping patients feel comfortable before, during, and after dental treatment
- Aiding in procedures that are part of dental treatment
- Providing diagnostic aids
- Sterilizing and disinfecting instruments and equipment
- Providing home-care instructions following oral surgical and similar procedures
- Preparing instruments and trays for dental procedures
- Maintaining records of treatment for patients
- Working on programs for control of plaque (a colorless film that forms on teeth)
- Assisting in prevention and management of dental and medical emergencies
- Setting up and maintaining such office procedures as appointments, payment schedules, infection control regulations, and supply inventories

Some dental assistants perform tasks that are similar to those of the dental technician, including making casts of the teeth and mouths from impressions, cleaning and polishing removable appliances, and making temporary crowns. Others prepare materials for impressions and restorations, take dental X-rays, and process X-ray film as directed by a dentist. They also may remove sutures, apply topical anesthetics to gums or cavity-preventive agents to teeth, remove excess cement used in the filling process, and place rubber dams on the teeth to isolate them for individual treatment. Each state regulates the procedures a dental assistant may perform, but the varied activities of an assistant in most states make for a challenging, interesting, and responsible position.

Work Settings and Hours

Most assistants work in private dental offices for dentists who practice individually or in a group practice, although assistants can also be found in a variety of settings, including dental specialty offices, hospitals, dental schools, or in any federal, state, or community clinic. Dental assistants may also choose to practice on armed forces bases, in educational and industrial settings, and in facilities for the disabled. In short, an assistant's skills are needed wherever people are practicing dentistry.

The type of work the assistant does and the responsibilities given to him or her in any of these practice settings may vary greatly depending on the culture of the office, the assistant's skills, and the dentist's disposition. Those who want greater responsibility should be sure to ask many questions of the person who interviews them for the job, including detailed questions about the nature of the work. In addition, expressing interest in gaining skills and additional on-the-job training will usually garner you greater responsibilities.

The work of an assistant in a general practice office depends on the size and nature of the practice. The assistant may be the only employee in a small practice. In those conditions, the assistant may answer the telephone, do the billing, schedule appointments, and help the dentist at chair-side. In a large practice, these duties are divided among several assistants. One may be the office manager who handles all records, schedules appointments, orders supplies, and is in charge of all business functions. Another assistant (or two) would work directly at the chair-side with the dentist and handle all instruments. In some offices, duties overlap, and assistants may be able to fill in at each other's jobs during lunch hours and vacations. In a busy office with one or more dentists, the ratio of assistants to dentists may be as high as five to one.

In the offices of dental specialists, duties of an assistant depend on the nature of the specialty. In orthodontic and pediatric practice, the assistant must work well with children and teenagers. In helping to provide endodontic and oral surgery treatment, the assistant's role resembles that of a surgical nurse, maintaining sterile conditions through the proper handling and sterilization of instruments. In oral pathology, the assistant must have knowledge of microscopic, biochemical, or other laboratory examination processes.

The choice of this career is not always a final one. The assistant may return to school to acquire additional skills and qualifications necessary to practice as a hygienist or dentist. Also, teachers are needed in the more than 250 training programs for dental assistants. Experience plus additional course work can lead to a career in education.

No matter what part of the assistant's career is most appealing, you should be sure that you enjoy people and are able to make them comfortable in what can sometimes be a tense situation. Because the assistant is often the first person to deal with the patient both in person and on the telephone, the initial impression is important. The way in which the assistant is able to relate to the patient may mean the difference between a pleased or dissatisfied patient.

Hours are usually as flexible as those of the dental hygienist, described in the previous section. With part-time hours, however, come few to no insurance benefits, which can be costly if paid out-of-pocket. Part-time or flexible hours are good for those currently in school or thinking about going back to school.

Employment Outlook

According to the U.S. Bureau of Labor Statistics, job prospects for dental assistants should be excellent in the upcoming decade. While dental assistants currently hold about 266,000 jobs, employment is expected to grow much faster than the average for all occupations through the year 2012. In fact, the job of dental assistant is expected to be one of the fastest-growing occupations, making this a fairly stable and secure field to enter. In addition to job openings due to employment growth, other factors include the need to replace assistants who transfer to other occupations, retire, or leave the labor force for other reasons. Finally, many of the opportunities available for dental assistants will be for entry-level positions.

Salaries for Dental Assistants

Dental assistants typically receive less compensation than the other positions discussed in this chapter. According to the U.S. Bureau of Labor Statistics, median hourly earnings of dental assistants were about $13.10 with the middle 50 percent earning between $10.35 and $16.20 an hour. The lowest 10 percent earned less than $8.45, and the highest 10 percent earned more than $19.41 an hour. This translates to approximately the low to upper $20,000 range per year. Salaries may vary from state to state with California cited as having the highest pay for health care providers, including dental assistants.

Dental Laboratory Technicians

The laboratory technician is the one person on the dental team who does not deal directly with patients. The technician spends the majority of his or her day in the laboratory, making a variety of appliances for the mouth, according to specifications outlined by the dentist. The lab typically includes an individual workbench with gas burners, grinding and polishing machines, and various hand tools. In many ways, dental laboratory technicians are like pharmacists; they fill prescriptions, but their prescriptions come from dentists and are for crowns, bridges, dentures, and other dental devices.

Dental laboratory technicians are also like sculptors; they craft objects using a variety of materials and tools. This work involves the construction of complete dentures and such small appliances as fixed bridges, removable partial dentures, crowns, inlays, and corrective appliances. The materials technicians work with include plastic, silver, stainless steel, wax, porcelain, and composite resins; every year new materials are being tried and tested for various appliances and prostheses. Trainees usually learn to work first in plaster and then graduate to more difficult materials.

Technicians' products aid patients' treatment. Appliances must fit correctly so that patients look and feel better; if the appliances don't fit perfectly, technicians may have to make adjustments. The typical way in which an appliance is made is as follows: first, dentists send a specification of the item to be manufactured, along with an impression (mold) of the patient's mouth or teeth. Then, dental laboratory technicians create a model of the patient's mouth by pouring plaster into the impression and allowing it to set. Next, they place the model on an apparatus that mimics the bite and movement of the patient's jaw. The model serves as the basis of the prosthetic device. Technicians examine the model, noting the size and shape of the adjacent teeth, as well as gaps within the gum line. Based upon these observations and the dentist's specifications, technicians build and shape a wax tooth or teeth model, using small hand instruments called *wax spatulas* and *wax carvers.* They use this wax model to cast the metal framework for the prosthetic device.

After the wax tooth has been formed, dental technicians pour the cast and form the metal and, using small hand-held tools, prepare the surface to allow the metal and porcelain to bond. They then apply porcelain in layers, to arrive at the precise shape and color of a tooth. Technicians place the tooth in a porcelain furnace to bake the porcelain onto the metal framework and then adjust the shape and color, with subsequent grinding and addition of porcelain to achieve a sealed finish. The final product is a nearly exact replica of the lost tooth or teeth that will fit precisely into the necessary space.

Technicians may choose to specialize in orthodontic appliances, crowns and bridges, complete dentures, partial dentures, or ceramics, or they may be generalists, performing the full range of skills. In some laboratories, technicians perform all stages of the work; in others, the different stages are assigned to different technicians. The size of the lab or dental practice will determine the skills needed.

Dental laboratory technicians possess talents and skills that are unique to the job, and these set it apart from other dental health care careers. If you plan to follow a career as a dental laboratory technician, you should possess fine motor skills, the ability to work with small devices and appliances, and attentiveness to detail. You should not mind working on your own and having limited contact with people, and you should be able to handle delicate objects without breaking them.

Work Settings and Hours

Dental laboratory technicians can work either in a dental office or in a commercial laboratory. The majority of jobs are in medical equipment and supply manufacturing laboratories, which usually are small, privately owned businesses with fewer than five employees. However, some laboratories are large; a few employ more than fifty technicians. Dental laboratories are located chiefly in large cities and states with large populations. Many laboratories fill orders for dentists who work far away and have no laboratory nearby. All work is done by following written instructions from dentists and using impressions of the patient's mouth made by the dentist.

Other work settings include dentists' offices, hospitals, government agencies, manufacturing firms, and self-employment. About a thousand dental laboratory technicians work in dentists' offices. For these technicians, written instruction is still given, but a problem in fitting or changing a denture or appliance can be solved while the patient is in the office. Hospitals and government agencies, such as the military services and the Department of Veterans Affairs hospitals, provide dental services to members and the public. In addition, firms that manufacture dental equipment often hire technicians as technical or sales representatives. These manufacturing firms also employ technicians to conduct research on new types of materials and equipment. Approximately one technician in seven is self-employed, a higher proportion than in most other occupations.

As in many other areas, teaching is also an option for dental laboratory technicians. There are more than fifty accredited programs for training dental laboratory technicians in the United States. Usually experience, rather than a degree, is the most useful factor in becoming an educator in this field.

The work hours for the dental laboratory technician are typically longer and more regular than those of other dental health care workers. Salaried technicians usually work forty hours a week. Self-employed technicians may have some flexibility in terms of when they work, but they're likely to work just as many hours per week to meet client demands and establish a dependable client base.

Employment Outlook

According to the U.S. Bureau of Labor Statistics, dental laboratory technicians hold about forty-seven thousand jobs throughout North America and there are additional positions available. Job opportunities for dental laboratory technicians are favorable, despite expected slower-than-average growth in the occupation through the year 2012. Employers tend to have difficulty filling trainee positions, probably because entry-level salaries are relatively low and the public is not familiar with the occupation, which is good news for those graduating from dental laboratory technician programs.

The demand for dental laboratory technicians' skills and the nature of the job have changed over the past several decades. As mentioned earlier, the dental health of the population has improved because of fluoridation of drinking water, which has reduced the incidence of dental cavities, and greater emphasis on preventive dental care since the early 1960s. As a result, the need for full dentures is decreasing, with increasing numbers of people needing only a bridge. However, during the last few years, demand has arisen from an aging public that is growing increasingly interested in cosmetic prostheses. For example, many dental laboratories are filling orders for composite fillings that are the same shade of white as natural teeth to replace older, less attractive fillings. This means that the future should be stable for dental laboratory technicians.

Salaries for Dental Laboratory Technicians

Data are limited, but past surveys show that, in general, wages for dental laboratory technicians were less than those for hygienists and assistants. Technicians in large laboratories tended to specialize in a few procedures and, therefore, tended to be paid a lower wage than those who were employed in small laboratories and performed a variety of tasks. According to the U.S. Bureau of Labor Statistics, the median hourly earnings of dental laboratory technicians were $13.70. The middle 50 percent earned between $10.51 and $18.40 an hour. The lowest 10 percent earned less than $8.16, and the highest 10 percent earned more than $23.65 an hour. Median hourly earnings of dental laboratory technicians were $13.78 in medical equipment and supplies manufacturing and $12.98 in dentists' offices.

4

OTHER DENTAL HEALTH CARE CAREERS

PREVIOUS CHAPTERS HAVE covered the most popular and well-known careers in dental health care. In this chapter you'll learn about other opportunities either directly in or related to dental health care. Websites are provided throughout the chapter so that you can conduct additional research on educational training required for each area and the salary you can expect to receive, as well as other details about the jobs. No matter which area of dental health care you ultimately choose to work in, you are sure to find satisfaction and opportunities aplenty.

Armed Services Opportunities

Many opportunities for the practice of any type of dentistry can be found in the U.S. armed forces. Indeed, there is always a demand for skilled dentists in the United States Army (www.army.mil),

Navy (www.navy.mil), Air Force (www.af.mil), and Marines (www .usmc.mil). Dentists who enter the armed forces are commissioned as captains in the army and the air force and as lieutenants in the navy. Graduates of dental schools are also eligible for federal civil service positions and for commissions (equivalent to naval lieutenants) in the United States Public Health Service.

The armed services are willing to train and educate those who enlist in these areas. The branches offer scholarships through the Armed Forces Health Professions Scholarship Program (HPSP), which pays for tuition and books and a provides a monthly stipend. In return, dental students will have an active duty obligation, which is one year of service for each year of scholarship support with a minimum of three years of active duty service. Scholarships are available annually from all service branches; you should contact the individual branches of service for more information. In addition, those who have been awarded grants from the Health Education Assistance Loan Program will not be required to repay their loans while they are serving in the armed forces.

Currently there are more than six thousand dentists in the U.S. Army, Navy, Air Force, Marines, and Public Health service. Dental health care providers are offered attractive incentives to become career officers in the uniformed services. Those who are employed in the civilian branches of the federal, state, and local governments are frequently compensated at a level approximating that of their colleagues in private practice. Other benefits of working for the federal government include an established practice, a highly trained staff, the chance to work in a variety of locations around the world, and not having to pay for malpractice insurance or balance the books. Keep in mind, however, that these perks come at a price, including having to move frequently, being in dangerous areas, and having little autonomy.

Public Service Careers

After completing the necessary training or education, a dentist, hygienist, assistant, or laboratory technician can use his or her skills in many different situations and settings to provide service to the public. Public service can include the Peace Corps (www.peacecorps .gov), with service inside or outside the United States. Inside the United States, the geographic area may be one in which there are not enough dentists or other dental employees to provide service to a given population, such as in impoverished rural or urban settings. For example, the Indian Health Service (www.ihs.gov), part of the U.S. Department of Health and Human Services, has dental teams working in remote parts of the United States to offer treatment to Native Americans living on reservations and to Alaska Natives. In addition, federal hospitals, prisons, and other remote facilities need to be served. Scholarships are available to those who volunteer to serve in these understaffed areas after they complete their training and education. (See Chapter 5 for more information.)

Many religious and charitable organizations maintain missionary dentists and assistants in remote areas of the United States and in other countries. The national organizations of Protestant and Catholic churches are responsible for staffing a large number of medical and dental missions. Knowledge of a foreign language can be a requirement for this work in an overseas assignment.

Dental Research

Dental researchers provide support for the work of the dental health care practitioner in proving or disproving the efficaciousness of treatment and technologies. Research covers a broad spectrum of activities, from high school students presenting at a science fair to dental school students in competition for a place at a national scientific session to professional scientists in search of answers about the cause of dental caries. People with all levels of education and experience working in a range of settings can make valuable contributions to the body of dental care knowledge.

History

As you can imagine, the development of the microscope and the discovery and use of radiographs were crucial to the progress of dental care. In the same way, the advances made in research today in improved materials, procedures, and instruments add to the efficiency and performance of those who care for patients. Experimentation and discovery will continue to result in improvements in dental treatment.

An outstanding researcher and pioneer in American dentistry was investigator and teacher Greene V. Black (1836–1915). Dr. Black did not attend a formal dental school but received his training through an apprenticeship; his ability to observe and study compensated for whatever lack of formal education he may have had. In addition to his Illinois practice, Dr. Black lectured on pathology, contributed articles to dental journals, and served as an officer in dental societies. He studied histology, chemistry, metallurgy, pathology, and dental processes. He educated himself in several of these fields by making microscopic slides of tissue. Visits to workers in fine metal—jewelers and clock makers—taught him how better to handle metals in the practice of dentistry. He invented a cord-driven, foot-powered dental engine and set up a shop for the manufacture and sale of these machines. In 1897, Dr. Black became dean of Northwestern University Dental School in Chicago, then one of the largest and most influential dental schools in the world. He continued to publish the results of his studies and experiments. His conclusions after many years of research in dental decay, filling materials, antiseptics, dental instruments, and many other topics are still honored and studied today.

Not all researchers and investigators have had the same impact in as many areas of dentistry as did Dr. Black, but other contributions have been valuable in establishing dental science. W. D. Miller (1853–1907), a friend of Black's, studied bacteriology and published results of his research to show that microorganisms are the cause of tooth decay. His book, *The Microorganisms of the Mouth*, was published in 1889.

Dental research was in its infancy at the turn of the century, but by the mid-1900s advancements were being made at a rapid pace, thanks to dental researchers. Dr. H. Trendley Dean was one of the first to investigate the benefits of fluoride; Dr. Robert Nelsen and his associates, who developed the high-speed dental hand piece; and Dr. Ray Bowen, who pioneered the use of new composite resins used for restorations of teeth. The National Institute of Dental Research, founded in 1948 to improve the oral health of the American people, supported the research on fluoride and fostered the rapid growth of dental research, both in scope and depth. (Today it's called the National Institute of Dental and Craniofacial Research and can be found at www.nidcr.nih.gov.) Currently, researchers are developing new technological methods for more efficient patient care: use of lasers in surgery, implants to replace damaged bone, and computerized or digital X-rays.

Major Research Organizations

There are two major national programs that contribute to dental research. The National Institute of Standards and Technology (www.nist.gov) focuses on developing new dental technology, tools, and materials while the National Institute of Dental and Craniofacial Research concentrates on research in biological sciences. In addition, research projects are carried out at the laboratories in the headquarters building of the American Dental Association and other major dental organizations.

In 1920, twenty-five members of the international community banded together to promote dental research by establishing the International Association for Dental Research (www.dentalresearch .org). This group publishes *The Journal of Dental Research* and holds annual meetings at which papers representing the most current findings are presented. The association has grown to include international divisions at which more than a thousand research papers can be given during a three- to four-day schedule.

Foundations and philanthropists have contributed to dental research through the establishment of programs such as the Gies Foundation in Washington, DC; the Eastman Dental Center in Rochester, New York; and the Zoller Memorial Clinic at the University of Chicago. Nearly all dental schools and colleges conduct continuing research programs.

During the 1940s, the federal government entered the field of dental research when the navy asked the National Research Council for advice on military dental standards. A dental advisory committee was formed to offer aid and approve grants. Shortly after, the Veterans Administration (now the Department of Veterans Affairs), the army, and air force began their own research programs. The National Research Council is now part of the National Academies (www.nationalacademies.org), which also comprise the National Academy of Sciences, National Academy of Engineering, and Institute of Medicine, all private, nonprofit institutions that provide science, technology, and health policy advice to the government.

The National Institute of Dental and Craniofacial Research (NIDCR) provides funds for research projects and fellowships for study at various dental institutions. It also provides training for those who are interested in basic sciences and helps other dental institutions set up research projects. The institute encourages each dental school to offer summer research awards to students. A dental student, hygienist, or assistant can complete a research project and report on it at a meeting of the American Association for Dental Research (www.aadrchicago.com) or the International Association for Dental Research. The NIDCR also involves many disciplines in the search for answers to problems that affect the mouth. For example, an investigation into the cause of caries can involve biochemists, nutritionists, geneticists, pathologists, and other scientists.

Research training is offered at nearly all dental schools as well as other institutions. Schools teach students to become familiar with the techniques, discipline, and procedures necessary to conduct scientific research. Training is offered at both the undergraduate and graduate levels.

Dental research provides support and essential background for practitioners in all of the dentistry disciplines. It is an area where workers interested in scientific methods and application of these methods can find employment. The ultimate benefit of research is to the dental patients, who are cared for by dental practitioners aware of and working with the latest advances.

Sales and Manufacturing

Other opportunities exist in dental-related positions in sales and manufacturing settings. Many manufacturers supply business forms, office furniture, dental chairs and attachments, laboratory equipment, instruments and accessories, restorative materials, and radiographic equipment. Sellers and manufacturers of the specialized equipment must have knowledge of dental procedures to produce, understand, and explain their products. Persons who are qualified in one type of dentistry, especially dental laboratory technicians, may move to the area of dental equipment, such as in manufacturing or sales.

Manufacturers of dental materials and equipment often conduct their own research through established programs that require the skills of experienced dental professionals, engineers, and researchers. Companies that produce toothpastes perform ongoing research in an attempt to improve their products. Similarly, companies that produce the materials used in dental fillings conduct controlled tests on these materials to check their long-term retention in teeth, their compatibility with tooth enamel, and their deterioration in the mouth. Gold was once used extensively as a filling material, but as the price of gold soared, manufacturers were forced to investigate new materials as a replacement. Also, as more practitioners treat disabled patients, engineers and dental professionals must develop new equipment to help these patients sit comfortably in a dental chair (rather than their wheelchair) and design special toothbrushes to help these patients best care for their teeth.

Dental Organizations

Nearly all state and regional dental societies have an executive director and staffs that vary in size depending on the size of the society. The American Association of Oral and Maxillofacial Surgeons (www.aaoms.org), the American Academy of Pediatric Dentistry (www.aapd.org), the American College of Prosthodontists (www.prosthodontics.org), the American Academy of Periodontology (www.perio.org), and many other national organizations maintain offices and staff that help run the group and disseminate information to group members. Staff may or may not need direct dental education depending on the job. In addition to their other work, many organizations produce professional journals related to their specialty, requiring the skills of writers and editors who have some dental care experience or knowledge. Web designers and content providers shape the official websites of these organizations. Finally, major organizations require marketing persons to help increase membership. See Appendix B for a listing of dental care organizations and their websites.

Education

Dental education is a broad field ranging from teaching in front of a class to writing educational booklets and brochures, to designing Web content for major organizations. Community colleges, universities, and graduate schools involved in dental education need teachers and administrators who are interested in sharing their knowledge with others. Local, state, and the federal governments employ knowledgeable persons to work on health care education programs that provide information to the public through newspapers, on the radio, and via television. If you have a flair for writing and communication and good people skills, you will likely do well in the educational sector. Keep in mind that many dental care professionals enter education after gaining some hands-on or clinical experience in the field. Also, you should note that there are opportunities for people from all aspects of dental care in education, including dental assistants, hygienists, and lab technicians, in addition to dentists.

Veterinary Dentistry

Unfortunately, oral and dental diseases are very common in animals. In fact, periodontal disease (gum disease) is the most common clinical condition veterinarians see when treating pets. It causes bad breath, pain, and reduced appetite, and it may affect various organs such as the kidneys, liver, and heart because of the introduction of bacteria into the system. As with people, good dental health in pets is a predictor of their overall health.

Veterinary dentistry is a small specialty within the field of veterinary medicine that has seen a growth in public recognition in recent years. As of 2004, only seventy-five professionals achieved diplomas in the specialty from the American Veterinary Dental College (www.avdc.org). Students of the college are not graduates of dental programs, but rather veterinarians attending school either full- or part-time seeking a diploma recognizing their expertise in this area.

The practice of veterinary dentistry is becoming more common and more sophisticated. Pets can have the same procedures as people, including root canals, crowns, and even braces! Veterinary dentists work with strange and exotic animals in addition to pets.

Those trained in veterinary dentistry perform routine dental cleanings, which consist of the following:

- Anesthetizing the animal and flushing the mouth with a solution to kill the bacteria
- Cleaning the teeth with handheld and ultrasonic scalers
- Polishing the teeth to remove microscopic scratches
- Inspecting each tooth and the gum around it for any signs of disease
- Flushing the mouth again with an antibacterial solution

- Recording any abnormalities or additional procedures on a dental chart
- Determining the best follow-up and home dental care program

There are several organizations dedicated to advancing this veterinary specialty and disseminating information about this growing field. The American Veterinary Dental Society (www.avds -online.org) is a major organization that also publishes the quarterly *Journal of Veterinary Dentistry*. The Veterinary Oral Health Council (www.vohc.org) oversees products manufactured to reduce animal periodontal disease and grants them a stamp of approval if they meet certain criteria. Finally, the Academy of Veterinary Dentistry (www.avdonline.org) is an international organization of veterinarians with a special interest in the dental care of animals.

Forensic Dentistry

Odontology is the branch of medicine dealing with the anatomy and development and diseases of the teeth. Forensic odontology applies the art and science of dentistry and dental knowledge to the solution of legal issues in civil and in criminal matters. It is a specialization of dentistry that helps identify victims in a death investigation through analysis of the victim's teeth and accompanying dental prosthetics, fillings, and compounds. In addition, forensic odontologists may analyze bite marks on a victim and match them to a perpetrator. Odontologists provide expert testimony in court involving criminal cases and civil dental issues such as personal injury law, workers compensation, professional malpractice, and disputes regarding aspects of the dentist/patient relationship. Those who work in this area of specialty must enjoy sleuthing, but it isn't a job for the faint at heart as the work can be quite grisly. In fact, identification of the human remains of natural disasters, terrorist activities, and missing and unknown persons is a major part of the job.

Forensic odontologists work with coroners, in a medical examiners office, for state and local government agencies, and in branches of the military. They may be permanently hired by these organizations or work on a contractual basis, receiving a fee for the services they provide. Sometimes odontologists provide consultation to insurance companies and legal firms.

The American Board of Forensic Odontology (www.abfo.org) is the credentialing body for dentists who have satisfied the experience and training requirements to sit for the ABFO examination. Training is in the form of courses and fieldwork designed to prepare the dental investigator to conduct thorough scientific and systematic scene investigations through use of approved techniques and methods.

You can find additional information about this area of forensic specialization from a variety of sources. Forensic Dentistry Online (www.forensicdentistryonline.org) is a fascinating website with tons of information for those interested in this field; it is filled with images, case studies, and online lectures on a variety of forensic topics. The American Society of Forensic Odontology (www.asfo .org) is an ideal source of information for anyone considering a career in odontology. The American Academy of Forensic Science (www.aafs.org) is the largest of its kind in the world. Holding annual meetings, it also publishes the *Journal of Forensic Science*. The International Organization for Forensic Odontostomatology publishes the *Journal of Forensic Odontostomatology*.

Now that you know about the kinds of jobs available to you in the dental health care field, it's time to learn about the education and training you'll need to land the job. The following chapter describes the education and training needed for the major areas of dental care, as well as how to finance your schooling.

5

EDUCATION AND TRAINING

PREPARATION AND RESEARCH are necessary steps to ensure you find satisfaction in a dentistry career and to guarantee you get into a good school. There are several things you can do to prepare yourself for entering dental school, some of which begin in high school. This chapter offers various tips for helping you choose a good school and making sure you're qualified to enter it. You will also read about ways to finance your education.

Preparation in High School

Preparing to enter dental school begins in high school, where you should take as many science courses as possible because basic sciences provide the foundation for more advanced biological, anatomical, and physiological college courses. In addition, if you are going to enter a dental career, it is important to find out as soon as possible if science appeals to you. Courses in biology, physics, chemistry, and advanced mathematics, in addition to English and humanities courses, are the most useful.

Another skill that will be invaluable is keyboarding. Throughout college you will need to prepare papers, educational materials, and a variety of other items; and later in your career, you will likely need to write business correspondence and professional papers. Keyboarding is a necessary skill to have since computers are such a pervasive part of any office or business setting.

As competition is keen for the number of places in dental school, you should try for high academic standards. Good grades, along with extracurricular activities, will help you get into a good program. Excelling in the sciences is also a good indicator of your potential to do well in a health field.

Determine Your Area of Interest

In late high school, early college, or during the course of your research on dental careers, try to determine the specialization or practice that interests you most. To get a better idea of the inner workings of the typical dental office, visit one to observe and ask questions of those working in the field. Ask if you can shadow someone for a day; most people will be flattered by your interest and pleased to show you what they do for a living. If you're shy about contacting someone, start by taking a closer look at the office the next time you go for your own dental appointment. In particular, notice the equipment and the various duties performed by the dentist, hygienist, assistant, and laboratory technician. Observe the teamwork of the personnel and who performs what tasks. While you are there, be sure to ask the dental professionals questions about their jobs, their training, and why they chose their professions. Most important, be sure to ask them if they like their jobs and to elaborate on the pros and cons of working in the field.

There are a variety of options in education after high school, once you determine your area of interest. In dental school, you have a choice of training for general dentistry or for one of the specialties of dentistry. Or, perhaps you find the teaching and patient education aspect of dental hygiene more appealing and decide to go that route. If you choose to become a dental assistant, you may decide that one of the specialties is more appealing than another and take extra courses in that field. Perhaps you find the business aspect more interesting, which means eventually taking courses to become an office manager. If you are considering training to become a laboratory technician, you can decide if you want to work independently, in a dental office, as part of a commercial laboratory, or for various governmental agencies such as the military services.

Research Educational Programs

Starting your junior year in high school, you should start researching dental programs. Many training programs and colleges have specific entrance requirements; knowing what they are well in advance will ensure you don't miss important deadlines. General requirements for admission to most colleges and universities include graduation from high school in the upper third or fourth of the graduating class and passing grades in a variety of specific courses. Scores from scholastic aptitude tests and other specialized tests will also be considered in your application, along with recommendations from teachers, your extracurricular activities, and personal qualifications.

High school counselors are a good resource for information on colleges and universities. They have a wide range of bulletins from many institutions for higher education that will give you information about the size of the school, the cost of attending, and the strengths of the school. Whether you prefer a small private school or a large state-supported program, the guidance counselor will have plenty of information for you.

As you research schools, whenever possible, you should visit the campus and talk to students in the school. Most colleges hold special visitation days when you can stay on campus and attend classes and social events. Guides are usually available to show you around and to point out the benefits of attending the institution.

Selecting a Dental School

Selection of a dental school depends on cost, location, size, and type of program offered. Degrees offered by the dental schools in the United States are the D.M.D. (Doctor of Dental Medicine) or the more traditional D.D.S. (Doctor of Dental Surgery). Today these two degrees are equivalent; they are simply different names for the same degree.

Accredited dental schools offer the best programs; each one is reviewed regularly and accreditation ensures high standards that include minimum requirements for the admission of students, recommendations and guidelines for courses to be included in the curriculum, financial stability of the institution, and qualifications of the faculty members. Dental schools also are members of the American Dental Education Association (www.adea.org). The association provides many services to individuals and institutions involved in dental education, including a continuing program of surveys of the needs of dental schools, faculty members, and students.

The goal of every dental school program is to produce graduates who are educated in biological and clinical sciences, capable of providing care to patients, and committed to high standards in their service. To produce these graduates, four years or more of study are required in the traditional dental schools. You may want to find out each school's specific requirements for graduation to assess whether it offers adequate clinical time and training. (See Appendix A for a list of dental schools in the United States and Canada.)

Accreditation

The Commission on Dental Accreditation of the American Dental Association (ADA) is responsible for granting accreditation status for all dental health care schools. Dental schools and programs listed as accredited have met the ADA's established standards and criteria for curriculum, faculty, and other factors. Association representatives visit schools and training programs regularly to ensure the standards are met. Indeed, the purpose of the entire accreditation system is to ensure high educational standards for students in the schools and training programs.

Applying to Dental School

After selecting the school or schools to which application will be made, you should obtain application materials either from the American Dental Education Association or from the school itself. Although application procedures vary from school to school, in general the application process begins about one year before the date of desired admission. Once the dental school has received the application, it will be screened and studied by an admissions committee. Most dental schools require that you complete at least two years of liberal arts study in college before entering a program, and some even require a baccalaureate degree. Other factors the committee reviews include biographical and academic information supplied by the applicant, his or her undergraduate education, letters of recommendation, and interviews. Interview policies vary widely among the schools; some schools require a personal interview, some make it an option for either the applicant or the admissions committee, and some give no interviews at all. Those applying to dental schools will have to take the Dental Admission Test (DAT).

Dental Admission Test

All U.S. dental schools require that applicants take the Dental Admission Test, administered by the American Dental Association (www.ada.org/prof/ed/testing/dat/index.asp). Dental schools apply different emphases to the test results, which are only one part of the admission process. The DAT is designed to assist the prospective student, his or her advisors, and the dental schools in evaluating the candidate's general academic abilities, comprehension of scientific information, and perceptual abilities.

The entire test is taken on computer and tests the following areas:

1. Knowledge of natural sciences (biology and inorganic and organic chemistry)
2. Reading comprehension (natural and basic sciences)
3. Verbal and quantitative ability
4. Perceptual ability (two- and three-dimensional problem solving)

There is no formal preparation for the test, although there are study materials available from the Dental Admission Testing Program (see website above or write to DAT Program, 211 East Chicago Avenue, 6th Floor, Chicago, IL 60611). Students who have not taken a basic science course in more than two years are advised to review for the test. You must have completed at least one year of college or university before you can take the DAT. You should plan on taking the DAT well in advance of applying to dental school, typically one year.

Curriculum

The majority of the first two years of dental school is spent in the study of biological sciences to learn about the function of the body and its diseases. The medical school faculty often provides instruction in the basic biological sciences. The dental school faculty is typically in charge of the more specific dental courses, such as oral anatomy, oral pathology, and oral histology.

During the first two years, the student also learns the basic principles of oral diagnosis and treatment. Students begin to practice on models of the teeth and mouth. In the final two years of dental school, students learn through clinical practice by treating patients under the supervision of clinical instructors. Clinical settings may be local hospitals or school-affiliated dental labs. Usually, students work in the various types of clinics of the dental school, moving from one type of dentistry to another. They learn the basic techniques involved in restorative dentistry, periodontics, oral pathology, orthodontics, pediatric dentistry, and other types of treatment that are part of a general dental practice. Students also learn to treat the chronically ill, handicapped, and older patients. In addition, most schools provide courses in practice management and effective use of assistants.

Curriculums in dental schools are constantly changing to stay current: new materials are introduced, new courses are given, and new techniques are developed. Some schools have adopted a four-academic/three-calendar-year curriculum. Recently, in clinical training, emphasis has been put on providing more comprehensive care for patients by recognizing additional needs and meeting these needs within the practitioner's level of competence.

For nearly all of the nine specialties in dentistry, additional study is required beyond the dental degree. (See Chapter 3 for additional information on educational requirements for some of the specialties.) Graduate programs offer specialized training with more time spent treating patients. Opportunities for learning in dental schools allow students many options in shaping their dental careers.

Education for Dental Hygienists

While schooling for dental hygienists is less rigorous than that for dentists, it is still fairly extensive and, depending on the school, may be difficult to attain because of high admissions standards. Nearly all dental hygiene schools receive more applications than can be accepted, so you should know the specific requirements of the school you hope to enter well in advance of applying to it. Some schools require a year or two of college prior to admission, while others require above average grades or experience in a dental office. In general, dental hygiene educational institutions may require the following of applicants:

- Have a high school diploma or GED certificate
- Be at least eighteen years of age
- Demonstrate good marks in math, chemistry, biology, and English
- Maintain a minimum of a C average in high school
- Have acceptable college entrance test scores (ACT, SAT)
- Complete prerequisite college courses in chemistry, English, speech, psychology, and sociology

Many dental hygiene programs additionally require a satisfactory score on the Dental Hygiene Aptitude Test. This test covers four areas of general knowledge: numerical ability, basic sciences (chemistry, physics, and biology), verbal ability and vocabulary, and reading comprehension. The examination is given throughout the year at various testing centers—usually at dental hygiene schools.

Curriculum

There is an array of educational options for those interested in becoming dental hygienists. In school, you may choose a two-year or four-year program. The two-year program leads to either a certificate in dental hygiene or an associate degree. If you wish to work in a clinic or a private office, the two-year program is typically adequate. The four-year program leads to a baccalaureate degree with a major in dental hygiene. If you would like a career in dental public health or in teaching or if you want to be more marketable, the four-year program is the better choice. Many schools offer a bachelor of science degree in dental hygiene, with both direct entry into practice and degree completion tracks for practicing dental hygienists who return to school for their degree. For advanced positions and for those who wish to enter research, many hygienists study for a master's degree, such as the M.S. (Master of Science) in dental hygiene education or administration, or the M.P.H. (Master of Public Health). In addition to taking classes on campus, there are online options for those interested in pursuing their dental hygiene education via computer or at remote learning sites. For those interested in other options in dental hygiene degrees, including online, degree completion, and master's degree programs, see the American Dental Hygienists' Association at www.adha.org.

Dental hygiene education consists of four areas of study: basic educational, basic science, dental science, and dental hygiene classes. Basic educational classes include English, speech, psychology, and sociology. Basic science classes may be chemistry, anatomy, physiology, biochemistry, microbiology, pathology, nutrition, and pharmacology. Dental science classes include dental anatomy, head and neck anatomy, oral histology, oral pathology, radiography, periodontology, pain control, and dental materials. Dental hygiene classes may include oral health education, preventive counseling, patient management, clinical dental hygiene, community dental health, medical and dental emergencies including basic life support, and legal and ethical aspects of dental hygiene practice. More or less education in any of these areas depends on the nature of the program.

Education for Dental Assistants

Until nearly thirty years ago, most dental assistants began their careers through on-the-job training, because few training programs were available. Today there are nearly three hundred approved schools that offer training courses. Courses in dental assisting are offered in many junior and community colleges, vocational and technical schools, or the armed services. (See the American Dental Association website for a list of accredited schools at www.ada.org.) Graduates of these programs usually receive certificates or associate degrees.

In the training schools for dental assistants, there are two types of programs: one-year programs award a certificate after successful completion and two-year programs offer a degree of Associate in Arts (A.A.) or Associate in Applied Science (A.A.S.). The ADA accredits mainly two-year programs offered at community colleges. Courses offered in the training schools include dental anatomy, nutrition, radiography, bacteriology, laboratory procedures, clinical practice, operating room procedures, and secretarial and office routines. Trainees can obtain practical clinical experience in affiliated dental schools, local clinics, or dental offices.

Unlike training and education for dentists, it takes a relatively short period of time to become a dental assistant. Most dental assisting programs take approximately nine to eleven months to complete. Additionally, there are a few programs available that feature accelerated courses, part-time programs for those currently working, and distance or online education, so there are plenty of options to meet your needs.

No specialized tests are given for admission to dental assisting programs, but most schools require a high school diploma or equivalency, above-average grades in science and English, a high school grade point average of C or higher, and a personal interview. Some programs require applicants to take a nationally recognized college entrance examination such as the School and College Ability Test (SCAT), the Scholastic Aptitude Test (SAT), or the American College Test (ACT). The SAT and ACT are administered annually at high schools in the United States. Those interested in taking the SCAT should talk to their high school or college career counselors.

Without further education, advancement opportunities are limited for dental assistants. Some go on to become office managers, dental-assisting instructors, or dental product sales representatives, while others go back to school to become dental hygienists. For many dental assistants, this entry-level occupation provides basic training and experience and serves as a stepping-stone to more highly skilled and higher paying jobs.

Education for Dental Laboratory Technicians

Most dental lab technicians pursue one of two avenues for training: on the job in a commercial laboratory or in a two-year educational program. In a commercial laboratory, the program usually lasts for approximately three years, depending on the student's ability to master various laboratory techniques. One benefit of this type of program is that the technician is paid during the apprenticeship period. In addition, once the training is finished, the technician receives a salary increase and has a job.

There are approximately twenty-five accredited programs in community colleges, technical institutes, vocational schools, and dental schools that provide instruction in the theory and principles of dental laboratory technology. (See www.ada.org for a list of accredited programs.) These programs provide classroom instruction in dental materials, oral anatomy, fabrication procedures, ethics, and related subjects. In addition, each student is given supervised practical experience in a school or an associated dental laboratory. Accredited programs normally take two years to complete and lead to an associate degree, although a few programs take up to four years to complete and offer a bachelor's degree in dental technology.

Graduates of two-year training programs need more hands-on experience to become fully qualified. Each dental laboratory owner operates in a different way, and classroom instruction does not necessarily expose students to techniques and procedures favored by individual laboratory owners. Students who have taken enough courses to learn the basics of the craft usually are considered good candidates for training, regardless of whether they have completed a formal program. Many employers will train someone without any classroom experience, and graduates of two-year programs typically spend less time training than those without. They may be more appealing to employers for just this reason.

The exact kind of curriculum varies depending on the institution, but, in general, most two-year programs, especially those that are accredited, are similarly structured. First-year courses typically include chemistry, dental law, metallurgy, laboratory techniques, and dental ethics. During the second year, students gain additional experience in the technology of working with small hand instruments, drills, and electrical equipment. They learn to construct dental appliances using a variety of materials, including plastic, gold, silver, stainless steel, and porcelain.

Unlike other dental care careers, students do not need to take a formal test or examination to enter dental lab technician training programs; instead, the basic requirement is a high school diploma. In considering candidates, employers or admissions personnel look for a high degree of manual dexterity, a well-developed sense of color perception, a concern for detail and accuracy, patience in working with small objects, and good grades in high school. High school courses in arts, metal and wood shop (industrial education), and basic sciences are most helpful if you are planning a career as a dental laboratory technician.

Financing Dental Education

Many prospective dental care students are concerned about financing their education, which can be quite expensive. Costs can range from $3,000 to $20,000 or more each year, depending on whether you attend a technical school or community college on the low end of the spectrum and colleges, universities, and advanced education in dental specialties on the upper end. Publicly supported schools are also less expensive than privately supported institutions. School tuition is not the only expense, however; students may also have to purchase instruments, books, and uniforms. Students who apply for admission to dental schools must be prepared to pay these costs.

The costs of the programs available for hygienists, assistants, and laboratory technicians vary considerably. Costs of education for dental hygienists can be nearly as much as dental school, if the student decides on graduate work. Obviously, the cost of the dental assistants' program is lower, as less time is required for training. Also, tuition at a community college can be as little as $30 to $50 for a course or as much as $8,000 for a fall semester at a college or university. Most of the approved training programs for laboratory technicians are at community or junior colleges, technical schools, or institutes, so the cost is much lower than that of attending a four-year program.

Although the costs of dental training are high, you should consider them a good investment for your future. At first, the expense of dental training may represent a sacrifice for both you and your family. But if you look at the investment of money as a source of increased income for you in the future, the cost seems worthwhile.

Holding a job while in school is difficult, if not impossible, depending on the program, so many students must seek additional sources of funding for their education. All schools have funds to provide financial assistance and will furnish information on the availability of that aid. Students should also investigate sources in their community. Service organizations, public and private loans, dental associations, state or federally guaranteed loans, and various types of scholarships can be useful sources of information and financial assistance. The following are some sources of financial aid.

Investigate Financial Aid

It's a good idea to investigate all types of financial aid available for training programs, and there are a variety of sources of financial aid if you spend some time searching for them. A good start is to meet with your school's vocational counselor and determine with your family and the counselor what resources are available to you. Many scholarship funds are overlooked because not enough people are aware of them. For example, there may be sources of aid in your own community through citizen groups or service organizations. There are also special government scholarships available for dental students if they provide public service after graduation. An online search using a variety of keywords, including "scholarship" and "dental" should yield a wealth of information. You can also obtain applications for loans and scholarships from the financial aid office of your desired school.

Federal Guaranteed Student Loan Program

The federal guaranteed student loan program makes it possible for students to borrow from private lenders to help pay the cost of school; the federal government pays part of the interest. Loans are guaranteed either by state or private nonprofit agencies or insured by the federal government. Undergraduate students may borrow up to $5,500 and graduate students $8,500 annually up to a total of $65,500. Repayment begins usually nine to twelve months after the student leaves school, but payment may be deferred for military or other service or additional study. Visit the U.S. Department of Education's Federal Student Aid website at http://studentaid .ed.gov for more information.

The Stafford Loan

The Stafford Loan is made by a lender such as a bank, credit union, or savings and loan association. The loans are insured by the guaranteeing agency in the borrower's state and typically have lower interest rates than other loans. Graduate students may borrow up to $18,500 a year for the entire period of graduate study, but they may not exceed an aggregate maximum of $138,000, including undergraduate loans. New borrowers pay up to 8.25 percent interest. A 3 percent origination fee is deducted from each loan payment and passed on to the federal government to help reduce the cost to the government of subsidizing the loans.

Repayment begins six months after the borrower leaves school or falls below half-time enrollment. The borrower must contact the lender to set up a repayment schedule, of which there are several types to choose from, including extended, fixed, and graduated payment plans. The borrower may have five to ten years to repay the loan, depending on the repayment schedule. Repayment can be deferred under certain circumstances, as when the borrower serves in the armed forces or for periods of unemployment, disability, or return to full-time study. In addition, these loans can be consolidated to achieve a lower interest rate. (See www.staffordloan.com for more information.)

PLUS Loans

PLUS loans are part of the guaranteed student loan program. These loans, made by banks, credit unions, and savings and loan associations, enable parents to borrow the entire cost of tuition, housing, and books, less other aid received, for each dependent child enrolled at least half time. This kind of loan is credit based, not needs based, which means anyone with good credit can get it. Repayment may be deferred under certain conditions, similar to those described previously. For more information, see www.plusloan.net.

National Health Service Corps Scholarship Program

The U.S. Department of Health and Human Services (http://nhsc .bhpr.hrsa.gov) sponsors scholarships that are available for dental students who are willing to give back to their communities. For each year of academic training during which students receive the scholarship, they must provide one year of public service in an underserved urban or rural community; a minimum of two years is required and you can get assistance for up to four years. Individuals are assigned to the National Health Service Corps, Indian Health Service, Public Health Service hospitals and clinics, U.S. Coast Guard medical facilities, federal prison medical facilities, or private practice in an understaffed area, depending on where they are most needed, so applicants must be flexible about where they can live and work.

Health Professions Student Loan Program

The U.S. Department of Health and Human Services also sponsors the Health Professions Student Loan program (http://bhpr .hrsa.gov/dsa/hpsl.htm). These loans have a low interest rate and can be made for as much as the cost of tuition plus $2,500 or more each year. Applications can be made directly from the dental school. Loans are repayable during a ten-year period that begins one year after a student stops full-time study at a dental school. Deferments are possible if a student joins the armed forces or the Peace Corps or begins advanced professional training. The federal government may repay part of these loans if the graduate practices in an underserved area.

Scholarships and Grants

There are a wide variety of scholarships and grants available to those who are willing to look for them. With some searching, everyone, but especially women and minority students, can find many awards and scholarships. Be sure to also check state dental societies, religious organizations, and the armed services. The following are just a sample of the different kinds of grants and scholarships available to dental health care students.

- AEF Air Force Spouse Scholarships
  (www.aef.org/aid/scholars.asp)
- American Academy of Implant Dentistry
  (www.aaid-implant.cnchost.com)
- American Association of University Women
  (www.aauw.org)
- American Association of Women Dentists
  (www.womendentists.org)
- American College of Prosthodontists Research Fellowships
  in conjunction with Proctor & Gamble
  (www.prosthodontics.org)
- American Dental Education Association
  (www.adea.org)
- Indian Health Service Dental Program
  (www.dentist.ihs.gov)
- National Health Service Corps Scholarship Program
  (http://nhsc.bhpr.hrsa.gov)
- Zeta Phi Beta General Graduate Scholarships
  (www.zphib1920.org)

If you choose to follow a career in one of the dental fields, with a bit of work, you can find some type of financial aid to help you attend school. All types of aid, especially that from a commercial lending institution, should first be investigated with the help of a vocational counselor at a high school or college. The financial aid picture is constantly changing, and it is absolutely essential to meet with financial aid counselors and vocational counselors regularly to keep up with changes in scholarship, grant, loan, and award-funding programs. The funding that was available last year may not be available this year, and new methods may have to be found.

6

Requirements for Practice

A DENTAL CAREER is a highly professional one. The eleventh edition of *Merriam Webster's Collegiate Dictionary* defines "professional" as "characterized by or conforming to the technical or ethical standards of a profession." The commitment to a dental career, whether as a dentist, hygienist, assistant, or laboratory technician, involves adopting the established professional standards of each field.

Dental health care professional standards have been set by members of four organizations: the American Dental Association (www.ada.org), the American Dental Hygienists' Association (www.adha.org), the American Dental Assistants Association (www.dentalassistant.org), and the National Association of Dental Laboratories (www.nadl.org). Each association has worked to establish such standards as licensing and certification, accreditation, codes of ethics, and continuing education. A look at some of these standards will help define the professionalism of a dental career. This chapter provides the information you need to ensure you meet your field's professional standards of licensure and certification, as well as practice.

Dental Associations

The people who work in the dental health care field have formed associations for the advancement of the both the profession and the practitioners of the individual dental specialties. The four main associations are discussed below.

American Dental Association

The American Dental Association was founded in 1859 by a small group of dentists meeting in Niagara Falls, New York. However, the group split as a result of the Civil War, when the Southern Dental Association was formed. In 1897 the two groups united to form the National Dental Association. In 1922 the association again assumed its original and current name, the American Dental Association.

The objectives of the association are to encourage the improvement of the health of the public, to promote the art and science of dentistry, and to represent the interests of the members of the dental profession and the public it serves. Its current membership includes some 150,000 dentists and students.

The American Dental Association headquarters is in Chicago and contains the administrative agencies, a dental library, and a two-floor laboratory complex. In addition, a number of national allied dental organizations are located in the building.

The association has an office in Washington, DC, that works closely with Congress and other governmental agencies in the Washington area. For example, the ADA cooperates with the National Institute of Dental Research, which is part of the National Institutes of Health. Association staff members also do research work at the National Bureau of Standards and the National Library of Medicine.

Benefits of membership in the American Dental Association include many scientific, professional, and consumer publications and insurance programs. Each year a comprehensive scientific session is held.

In addition, the councils and bureaus of the association provide these services to members and to the public: formulating requirements for accreditation of educational programs, providing community dental health programs, evaluating dental materials and products, advising on laws relating to dental health, supplying data and statistics about the dental profession, and performing research in areas such as biochemistry, pharmacology, biology, and dental materials.

American Dental Hygienists' Association

A group of about fifty hygienists organized the American Dental Hygienists' Association at a meeting in Cleveland, Ohio, in 1923. By 1927 the association had 467 members. Growth of the association was slow during the depression years, but in the 1940s two factors contributed to a faster pace: during World War II, the military forces began accelerated programs for training dental hygienists, and more training programs were set up in technical institutes.

By 1960 there were thirty-seven training programs; the primary setting was the community college. The association worked to maintain high levels of education. By the end of the 1960s, nearly eighteen thousand hygienists were employed.

A major achievement of the association is setting and maintaining educational standards. The association (with the American Dental Association) provides continuing education for the practicing dental hygienist. The association helps the hygienist keep up-to-date through publications, scientific sessions, workshops, films, and tapes.

The association also provides a variety of insurance programs, a professional journal and a monthly news magazine, dissemination of information, and promotion of legislation that affects dental hygienists. The association headquarters are located in Chicago.

American Dental Assistants Association

The American Dental Assistants Association was founded in 1925 by Juliette Southard at a meeting in Dallas, Texas. The headquarters office is in Chicago, where all activities are coordinated. The association has held annual meetings since the first one in Texas. This is one of many services offered to members.

Education has been a major concern of the association. In 1940 its education committee provided the first study course outline for dental assistants. During the 1940s, programs were established at vocational, technical, and community schools; today's total is more than 250 such programs.

The association has established a certifying board that requires that dental assistants participate in continuing education to maintain certification. Any assistant who wishes to write the initials C.D.A. (Certified Dental Assistant) after his or her name must be a graduate of an accredited program, pass a written examination, and provide proof of professional ethics. After earning the initial certification, the assistant must obtain at least twelve hours of continuing education each year.

The association offers a variety of insurance plans to its members, provides scholarships, prepares clinics, and offers many opportunities for the exchange of ideas, including a monthly journal.

National Association of Dental Laboratories

In the early 1900s, several dental laboratory groups were formed to establish ethical standards for the industry and to represent the industry in its dealings with members of the dental profession, the dental trade organization, and the federal government.

In 1933 the government ruled that, as an industry, dental laboratories must be operated by a code of fair practices, and a group was organized to formulate these practices.

In 1951 the National Association of Dental Laboratories was formed at a meeting in Chicago. In 1958 the association established the Certified Dental Technician (C.D.T.) program, which is intended to raise the overall performance of the dental laboratory industry and craft and to provide continuing advanced education to its practitioners.

The association works closely with organized dentistry at national and state levels. Its members are encouraged to provide services of a high quality to the dental profession in accordance with state laws.

In 1977 the association established a voluntary national program of certification of dental laboratories in which a framework is set for upgrading laboratory facilities and personnel. In the first year, the voluntary program brought in more than a hundred laboratories; many others indicated their support for the program.

There is no national organization for individual laboratory technicians; however, those technicians who are part of the C.D.T. program receive several services and benefits. These include access to group life insurance programs, subscriptions to professional and technical journals, and participation in a variety of study group programs.

There is, however, a professional association for dental laboratories in general, called the National Association of Dental Laboratories. For more information go to www.nadl.org.

The aim of these four associations and that of many other organizations within the dental health care field is to provide well-trained professional workers who can offer the best dental care.

Additional Professional Associations

In addition to the American Dental Association, the American Dental Hygienists' Association, the American Dental Assistants Association, and the National Association of Dental Laboratories, there are virtually dozens of other professional associations covering the variety of specialties within dentistry and dental care. Their names, such as Academy for Implants and Transplants or American Academy of Pediatric Dentistry, reveal their focus. Making contact with the organizations that interest you, through a phone call, letter, e-mail, or a visit to their website, will provide you with additional career information. A complete list is provided for you in Appendix B.

Licensure and Certification

Licensure and certification are necessary to protect the health, safety, and welfare of the public and to ensure standards of competency. Requiring licensure and certification ensures that only trained and qualified professionals are practicing in each field and it provides a means of keeping track of those who fulfill their requirements and those who are unfit to practice. Not all dental health care fields, however, require licensure. Those that do typically require an examination designed to assess a graduate's ability to understand information from basic biomedical and dental sciences and apply that knowledge in a problem-solving context. In essence, it evaluates the candidate's competence.

Dental Licensure

A government agency must approve a dentist's qualifications before he or she can legally treat patients. The process by which a government agency approves the dentist's qualifications is called dental licensure; the credential awarded is a dental license. Individual states, districts, and dependencies award dental licenses, so a license awarded by one area permits the recipient to practice only in that location. For example, dentists licensed in Illinois cannot practice in New York until they obtain a license from New York. The government agency that issues dental licenses is usually the state board of dental examiners.

Licensure requirements vary from state to state, but all are similar in some respects; they consist of an educational requirement, a written examination requirement, and a clinical examination requirement. Graduates of programs accredited by the Commission on Dental Accreditation of the American Dental Association meet the educational requirement. For written examinations, most states recognize the results of the National Board Dental Examinations. (See www.ada.org for more information.) The clinical examination requirement falls under the auspices of the state board of licensure or a regional dental testing agency. All candidates for licensure must pass a clinical examination in which specific procedures must be performed. Usually the candidate must supply the necessary instruments and bring a patient needing the prescribed treatment. Finally a licensing jurisdiction may also require candidates to be of sound moral character; this documentation may vary from state to state. Many jurisdictions require proficiency in conversational English.

The Joint Commission on National Dental Examinations of the American Dental Association administers the National Board Dental Examinations program. There are eleven National Board examinations: Part I includes four tests of knowledge about basic sciences and dental anatomy; Part II includes seven tests on dental specialties and pharmacology. Part I takes a full day to complete; Part II takes about a day and a half. The computerized exam consists of multiple-choice questions and is offered nearly every day of the year at designated testing centers. Written exams are only offered a few times a year and may eventually be phased out by the computerized exams. Students can become familiar with the test items by purchasing old copies of the test through the American Student Dental Association (see www.asdanet.org for more information).

Dental Hygienists' Licensure

Similar to dentists, dental hygienists must also obtain a license before practicing. After graduation from an accredited program, the hygienist candidate must take the written National Board Dental Hygiene Examination, which consists of tests on basic sciences; dental anatomy, histology, and pathology; pharmacology; nutrition; dental materials; radiology; and preventive dentistry. The candidate must also pass a state or regional clinical (practical) examination.

The candidate must pass both the written and clinical examinations and be licensed by the State Board of Dental Examiners in the state selected for practice. Most states accept the National Board Dental Hygiene Examination for the written tests; those that do not provide their own written examinations. The Joint Commission on National Dental Examinations, under the ADA, is also responsible for this test. Regional examining boards, which include a group or an area of states, have established clinical tests accepted by the groups. Many states also require a written test on the State Dental Practice Act to ensure applicants are knowledgeable of their state's laws and the scope of their practice within the state. After all tests are successfully completed, the hygienist is classified as R.D.H. (Registered Dental Hygienist).

The rapid growth in the scope of dental hygiene has led some states to require that candidates be tested in new procedures for which they may be responsible. These may include placing, polishing, and removing temporary and other restorations; performing gingival curettage (surgical cleaning); administering anesthesia; and other functions. In many states, an additional requirement for continued licensure is that a certain number of continuing education credits be earned each year.

Dental Assistants' Certification

The dental assistant is not licensed but certified. Requirements for certification include graduation from an accredited dental assisting program and successful completion of the certification examination of the Certifying Board of the American Dental Assistants Association. The examination is not a requirement for practice but is taken voluntarily to verify the assistant's competence. The written test covers theory and knowledge of laboratory methods and techniques, basic and dental science, radiology, and functions of the assistant. Standard clinical procedures are also part of the examination.

After the examination is successfully completed, the assistant holds the title of Certified Dental Assistant (C.D.A.). By participating in a continuing education program, the assistant can continue to achieve certification status annually. As the duties of assistants expand, licensure or registration of all dental assistants in every state may become a reality.

Dental Laboratory Technicians' Certification

The certification program for technicians was founded in 1958 by the National Association of Dental Laboratories in cooperation with the Council on Dental Education, American Dental Association. The program, according to the National Association of Dental Laboratories, is designed to bring recognition to the highly qualified, ethical dental technician, provide continuing advanced educational opportunities, and raise the overall technical and ethical performance standards of the dental laboratory industry and craft.

Candidates for the Certified Dental Technician (C.D.T.) designation must take a written examination that covers history, ethics, and jurisprudence in the dental laboratory industry, plus techniques, procedures, and materials needed in laboratory specialties. Tests consist of multiple-choice questions. Candidates must also prepare preliminary laboratory work, which they bring to the examination. Those who sign up for the test will receive instructions and materials approximately four weeks before the testing session.

C.D.T. candidates must have a high school education or equivalent and five years of experience to sit for the test. Candidates may substitute time spent in approved supervised training in a dental laboratory school for part of the experience requirement. Certified dental technicians must renew their certification every year by meeting continuing education requirements and must attest to their continuing ethical standards.

Ethics and Professional Conduct in Dentistry

Another means to ensure high standards for the dental profession is to establish codes of conduct for its members. The Principles of

Ethics and Code of Professional Conduct of the American Dental Association is an ever-evolving document that describes the ethical and professional obligations dentists have with their patients in particular and society in general. This in-depth description of the profession's highest standards is composed of three main parts: the Principles of Ethics, the Code of Professional Conduct, and the Advisory Opinions. The Principles of Ethics provides guidance for dentists in their conduct and are composed of the following five ethical principles: patient autonomy (self-determination), nonmaleficence (doing no harm), beneficence (doing good), justice (fairness), and veracity (truthfulness). The Code of Professional Conduct, a result of the ADA's legislative efforts, provides guidance on conduct that is either expected or prohibited. Professionals who violate the code may receive disciplinary action and suspension of their license. The Advisory Opinions are interpretations of the code as it applies to certain situations. The ADA's Council on Ethics, Bylaws, and Judicial Affairs generates the Advisory Opinions for the purpose of providing guidance to dental professionals.

The Principles of Ethics and Code of Professional Conduct define and describe how dentists should practice. For example, dentists who announce themselves as specialists must have successfully completed an accredited educational program and have received a diploma from a recognized certifying board. The scope of the individual specialist's practice is governed by the educational standards for the specialty. The practice carried on by dentists who announce as specialists must be limited exclusively to the special area(s) of dental practices announced by the dentist. Similarly, general practitioner dentists can announce the availability of their services so long as they do not express or imply specialization. Advertising services that are in the domain of specialists can open the general practitioner up to legal prosecution. Every dentist should be familiar with the ethical and professional standards of the field to provide the best possible care. You can download a copy from the ADA's website.

Code of Ethics for Dental Hygienists

Similar to the ADA's code for dentists, the American Dental Hygienists' Association's (ADHA) stated purpose of a professional code of ethics is to achieve high levels of ethical consciousness, decision-making, and practice by the members of the profession. Each member of the ADHA has the ethical obligation to subscribe to the following principles:

- Provide oral health care utilizing the highest professional knowledge, judgment, and ability
- Serve all patients without discrimination
- Hold professional patient relationships in confidence
- Seize every opportunity to increase public understanding of oral health practices
- Generate public confidence in members of the dental health professions
- Cooperate with all health professions in meeting the health needs of the public
- Recognize and uphold the laws and regulations governing the dental hygiene profession
- Participate in the ADHA and uphold its purpose
- Maintain professional competence through continuing education

- Exchange professional knowledge with other health professions
- Represent dental hygiene with high standards of personal conduct

Visit the ADHA's website at www.adha.org to read the entire Code of Ethics for Dental Hygienists.

Principles for Dental Assistants to Follow

The American Dental Assistants Association (ADAA) sets the standards of practice for dental assistants, which is an increasingly well-organized and professional field. The mission of the ADAA is "to advance the careers of dental assistants and to promote the dental assisting profession in matters of education, legislation, credentialing and professional activities which enhance the delivery of quality dental health care to the public." According to the Principles of Ethics and Code of Professional Conduct of the American Dental Assistants Association, every member is required to adhere to the following obligations:

- Keep confidential the details of the professional services provided and the confidences shared by any patient
- Seek continuing education to maintain and improve proficiency in skills and abilities
- Participate in the activities of the ADAA to improve the educational and professional status of dental assistants
- Refrain from performing any service for patients that is outside the scope of practice

- Support the Statement of Professional Commitment: "As a professional dental assistant, I will promote the advancement of the careers of dental assistants and the dental assisting profession in matters of education, legislation, credentialing and professional activities which enhance the delivery of quality dental health care to the public."

You can go to the ADAA's website at www.dentalassistant.org for more information.

Practice Objectives for Dental Lab Technicians

The National Association of Dental Laboratories (NADL) has certain objectives that members are expected to adhere to, including the following:

- To advance dental lab technicians' standards of service to the dental profession and to establish cooperation among members of the field
- To encourage high standards of integrity, honor, and courtesy by disseminating technical knowledge and information among members of the industry
- To encourage the formation of additional state, local, and regional dental laboratory associations and coordinate activities with those of existing organizations
- To encourage strict compliance with all laws relating to the regulation of dental technology and assist in the adoption of new laws as needed to promote the best interests of the public
- To assist members in the interpretation of all government decrees, orders, rules, and regulations applicable to the field of dental technology

- To assist in the education and training of all those engaged in the dental prosthetic art and science
- To engage in research to further the science and technical aspects of the field and advance it as a profession

Visit www.nadl.org for more information on the association's bylaws, policies, and procedures.

Continuing Education

An important part of the professionalism of any career is the desire to keep gaining knowledge. For all phases of dentistry, new techniques, methods, and materials are continuously being developed, requiring the dental health care professional to keep up to date. One of the most effective ways to stay abreast of advances in dental technology is through continuing education.

Courses in continuing education are offered through many different institutions and in many different settings and formats. The four main dental health care associations featured in this chapter—ADA, ADHA, ADAA, NADL—frequently sponsor programs. Continuing education is offered in the form of classes at a university or community college, in study groups, at conferences, in hospitals, and at association-sponsored events. Courses can be one-day or all-day sessions or seminars that continue for several weeks and range in subject matter from practice management to infection control techniques to patient management. Other continuing education options also include online study and reading articles from a professional journal, such as the *Journal of the American Dental Association.*

Anyone truly interested in maintaining a professional attitude will want to take part in an educational experience that will increase skills and ability and will ultimately benefit patients' dental health.

Additionally, continuing education is a requirement for maintaining valid licensure and certification, although the amount varies from state to state. In today's fast-paced, highly technological world, it is necessary to stay current to provide the best care and have marketable skills.

Professional Liability Insurance

A malpractice lawsuit can be brought against anyone working in the dental health care field, including dental assistants and hygienists. As a future dental professional, your skills and experience will be regularly tested in emergency situations, under stressful conditions, and with difficult patients. Unfortunately, something may go wrong or the patient may perceive that you were negligent, in which case you may end up facing a malpractice suit. A charge of negligence could render the unfortunate dental professional penniless and could mean the end of a career. This is why all health care professionals are required to have liability insurance to practice in our highly litigious society.

Professionals are expected to have extensive technical knowledge or training in their particular area of expertise. They are also expected to perform the services for which they were hired, according to the standards of conduct in their profession. Thus, the more training you have, the better off you are. With more education you are better prepared to make decisions. Certified dental lab technicians, for example, are considered more reliable and less of a risk than those without certification.

Professional liability insurance is a specialty coverage, which means that dentists must have dental liability insurance whereas nurses must have nursing liability insurance. Legal fees and court costs incurred by the insurer on your behalf are paid for covered claims, in addition to the liability limits, even if the suit is groundless, false, or fraudulent. You will not have to worry about suffering from the expense of a lawsuit brought on by someone who is only interested in suing for the money if you have liability insurance.

Some associations offer additional liability insurance for members. The ADAA provides dental assistants with a Professional Liability Policy that covers most members against claims arising from professional services provided by the dental assistant. In most cases, however, the dental assistant will be provided coverage under the malpractice policy of the dentist who supervises the care and treatment being provided. However, if the overseeing dentist does not have insurance coverage or another issue arises that causes the dental assistant not to be provided with coverage, the ADAA Dental Assistant Professional Liability Policy provides a safety net for its members. Many types of insurance plans—including life, medical, and liability—are available. You must seek advice and compare plans before deciding on the best package for your needs.

7

STARTING YOUR CAREER

CONSIDERING THE SATISFACTIONS and rewards of a dental career is just one part of the process of determining whether dental health care is the right field for you; taking the time to evaluate your personal qualifications is another important step. An honest evaluation of your personal merits and motivations can help you make a more informed career selection. As you read this chapter, try to determine whether you possess many of the qualities discussed to assess your likelihood of meeting the goal of a dental career.

In addition to assessing your skills and talents for doing the work of dentistry, this chapter offers tips and techniques for finding the best jobs. There are a variety of resources for locating jobs; all require a certain amount of perseverance. From online to print sources, this chapter gives you the information you need to further research the kinds of jobs available and how much they pay.

Personal Motivations and Strengths

No one possesses every skill and strength found in all the best dental health care workers. Indeed, most people who will go on to have successful careers may only possess the majority of them or they may have some and learn to develop others through training and education. Regardless, understanding what traits make for a successful work life can be a good way to evaluate your potential for enjoying a fruitful career in this area. The following are the personal motivations and strengths that help one excel in the dental health care field:

- **Commitment to a goal.** You should be able to determine which part of dentistry appeals to you and have specific steps to achieve that goal.
- **Willingness to train.** You must be able to take orders from others, especially during a training period, both in school and on the job.
- **Interest in science.** All areas of dentistry require knowledge, enthusiasm, and curiosity about science—ranging from basic sciences to the details of research.
- **Ability to work hard.** In many instances, you may have to work irregular hours with time extending longer than a forty-hour week. Certainly, in your school or training program, long hours of work plus study will be necessary.
- **Concern for people.** In dentistry, patients will need your reassurance and concern about the state of their oral health. If you are not genuinely caring, you may not want to consider a career working with patients in a health-oriented profession.

- **Achievement in scholarship.** You must be able to achieve grades that are above average to be accepted in an accredited program. If you establish good study habits, you should be able to attain the necessary grades.
- **Dexterity in manual skills.** Part of the Dental Admissions Test identifies factors in perceptual ability that predict manual ability. While all dental schools require candidates to take it, the test results are only one factor considered in evaluating the admission potential of a candidate. You can check your ability by working with hand tools to create a small model in wood, plaster, clay, or any similar material.
- **Ability to communicate.** Communication is vital in all aspects of dental health care. You communicate with your voice, body language, and facial expressions. You must be aware of how best to deal with each patient's needs and how to respond to these needs through good communication.
- **Continued desire to learn.** Every job in the field of dentistry requires continual education on new developments and technologies, which will benefit the profession and the patients it serves.
- **Cooperation with others.** Getting along with people on all levels is an important asset to any career, but this is especially true in dentistry. Join groups in which you can interact with your peers or with people older or younger than yourself to sharpen this skill.

Psychology of Dentistry

In analyzing your motivations for entering dentistry, you are engaging in a psychological self-examination. Psychology needs a separate section of its own in this chapter because of its importance in dental care. Psychology can be defined as a study of the mind and behavior; this knowledge is essential to those who want to practice in dentistry both in terms of dealing with a range of personality types and in combating the fear of dentistry.

Dentistry by its nature is extremely personal. Physical closeness is inevitable as members of the dental care team provide treatment. Dealing with people at close range means that you must be aware of the sensitivities of patients and provide treatment with concern for their mental well-being, in addition to the physical state of their teeth.

Many patients arrive at the dental office in a state of apprehension. The chief reasons for patients' anxiety about visiting the dentist's office are lack of communication between the dentist and patient, perceived lack of control while in the dentist's chair, and fear of being criticized for not taking care of their teeth. Patients may be nervous because of a previous painful experience or because they are in pain and need treatment. People also believe that they will inevitably lose their teeth as they grow older; this has come to be accepted as part of the aging process. Developing positive attitudes about dentists and receiving dental care in the midst of all these negative feelings is difficult.

You can trace dental phobias and the general apprehension many feel when going to the dentist to a variety of factors, some of which are associated with painful or traumatic events that often go back to childhood. Some begin to associate anything to do with the mouth with pain when they are a child and their teeth come in—a painful process in itself. Loss of primary teeth or accidental injury also causes great pain. If the appearance of the first cavity in the mouth is associated with a trip to the dentist where the child is told that all the sugar-containing foods he or she enjoys are bad for the teeth, it follows that the dentist is someone to be avoided. These negative feelings can carry over to adult life and habits.

Even today, not enough people think of the dentist as a person who provides preventive care. The dentist is associated with removal of teeth, drilling, anesthetics, and repair, rather than with comfort and ease of pain. The treatment is also regarded as expensive, and many people use this as an excuse for not visiting the dentist regularly. Thanks to the dental profession's emphasis on preventive care and good oral hygiene, plus the fluoridation of water, impressionable children and people in general have fewer cavities than they did twenty years ago. The new technological advances—high-speed dental drills, anesthetics, and antibiotics—also make dental care quite painless, which means less chance of negative feelings consistently associated with visits to the dentist.

There are many methods for treating fearful patients. Behavioral techniques for treating this anxiety include patient relaxation, systemic desensitization, hypnosis, and meeting with the patient in a nonclinical setting to discuss the patient's concerns. A number of universities, medical centers, and hospitals have clinics to treat dentally anxious patients. If psychology is not a requirement in your training program, you should put it at the top of your list of electives. To overcome the patient's negative images and feelings, the dentist and staff members must use certain techniques to effect a change in attitude. The following sections describe some general techniques that any professional dealing with patients can study and apply in a professional setting.

Technical Skills

Dental professionals acquire and fine-tune technical skills during the clinical portion of education and training. While in school, there is generally ample time to hone these skills. When the dental professional enters practice, he or she must be adept at not only performing the technical skills, but also explaining them in a reassuring and nontechnical way to the patients. A patient who not only believes that the professional is well qualified but also understands the procedures he or she is about to undergo will be more likely to relax.

Effective Communication

The most important technique for dental professionals to acquire is effective communication. Each patient brings to the dentist's office a different set of emotions and motivations. Some patients can be given a logical explanation for their proposed treatment; others need a more emotional response.

In the communication process, the dental professional must quickly assess the patient to determine the best approach for dealing with him or her, and this involves listening while the patient expresses his or her needs. For example, with patients who are concerned about cost, dental professionals may need to explain treatment in terms of the amount of money the patient will save over a period of time. For those concerned primarily with appearance, the professional emphasizes the aesthetic appearance of their teeth. For those with a fear of losing control, the dental professional can explain that if the patient raises his or her hand, the professional will immediately cease treatment.

Patient Involvement

To motivate a patient to overcome fears and apprehensions and use preventive dentistry practices, the dental staff must find the right approach and a logical one does not always work. People may be aware of the causes of dental decay but may not follow preventive procedures any more than they consistently fasten seat belts in automobiles. So, how does the dentist know what is the right approach?

The right approach is the one that appeals to the patient. Often, participation will work. If the patient can brush or floss while the hygienist is explaining the technique, the lesson will be reinforced. Visual reinforcement with pictures and drawings is also appealing to patients, especially to those who are visual learners. Emphasize the effects of oral disease. Offer immediate and long-term goals for the patient to achieve. Put the patient in first place; it is the patient, not the dentist, who is the prime provider of dental health. Emphasize the outcome—an attractive smile.

Preparing to Start Your Career

Job-hunting can be an intimidating process, but it can be less so if you're well informed. During college you should start to prepare to launch your career in dental health. This section describes how to find the best jobs and make yourself the most appealing candidate.

Subscribe to Professional Journals

Besides being a good source of information about the latest advancements in the field, professional journals can also tell you a lot about the types and location of job opportunities across the country. Most professional journals contain classified advertising, usually at the back of the magazine. These ads often describe the jobs, benefits, and compensation. Each area of dentistry has at least one journal devoted to the interest group, for example: *Dimensions of Dental Hygiene* (www.dimensionsofdentalhygiene.com), *The Dental Assistant* (www.dentalassistant.org), *Journal of Dental Tech-*

nology (www.nadl.org), the *Journal of the American Dental Association* (www.ada.org), and *Mouth* (journal of the American Student Dental Association, www.asdanet.org). Do an online search using keywords to locate these and many other helpful magazines and journals.

Register with a Placement Officer

Nearly every college and training program has a placement officer or a full-time staff person who can help you find a position in your field of interest. Some placement offices act as a service to send transcripts and other records for you. Other placement offices post announcements of available positions and keep students informed about vacancies that occur, both in nearby communities and in other states. Dentists consider reputable programs to be good sources of potential applicants, and many call or write to the placement officer when a position is available.

Establish References

Most employers require references before hiring prospective employees because they help in making the decision to hire a person based on their past performance. References are either current or past supervisors or college professors. Never offer a name for reference unless you have first asked permission to use that person's name. Be sure the person you ask is a responsible person who knows you well and will respond quickly to a request for a reference.

Placement services and some college career offices keep letters of reference on hand for you. If you are using a placement service, a written general reference can be copied as needed to send to prospective employers. In this way, only one copy of each letter of reference is needed.

Preparing Your Résumé and Cover Letter

Your résumé is one of the most important items you may ever prepare. It gives employers their first look at you, and its neatness and thoroughness make the initial impression. An attractive résumé is minimally designed and printed on high-quality, white or cream paper with no errors.

The résumé should contain your personal history in a chronological order. It should present your education, work experience, goals, personal data, special interests, awards and accomplishments, and one or two references or the phrase "References Available Upon Request." Ideally, the résumé is on one sheet of paper that has your name, address, phone number, and e-mail listed at the top of the page. For most students just out of school and with little on-the-job experience, the résumé will highlight courses taken—in particular, clinical courses—and academic achievements. In some cases, you may have to slightly change your letter of application and résumé according to the type of position you are seeking.

You can create a general cover letter and customize it for each position to which you will apply. In every cover letter you send out, be sure to include information about yourself that demonstrates you are qualified for the position; express yourself in such a way that shows you are self-confident, but without being self-centered. Indicate your desire for an interview, and be sure to tell the person to whom you're writing that you'll follow up your letter with a phone call. Be sure also to include in your cover letter a statement of flexibility, such as a willingness to work nontraditional hours or to substitute—it will make you more marketable—and ask that your résumé be kept on file in case of future openings. Include a copy of your résumé with every cover letter you send out, and be sure that all of your contact information is in your cover letter.

The Job Hunt

After you have completed your degree or finished your training, it's time to find a job; and with job hunting, organization is key. Begin by organizing the materials necessary for job hunting. Have copies of transcripts, awards, letters of application, and your résumé neatly organized so you can find them quickly, and send copies as needed. Be sure to keep copies of all your cover letters and correspondence, including a phone log, so that you know who has expressed interest and when it's time to follow up a letter with a phone call.

Occasionally the perfect job will fall right into your lap, but usually dental care professionals must take an active role in seeking a new position. Here are some avenues to pursue in your job hunt.

Newspapers

Only about 20 percent of jobs are found through want ads in newspapers. However, employers who advertise jobs in newspapers often use a "blind ad" when looking for new employees, which requires that you respond to a post office box. This allows the dentist to remain anonymous and puts the job applicant at a distinct disadvantage. You might find yourself applying for positions you don't want. If you are already employed, you may be sending a résumé to someone whom you would rather didn't know your intentions. However, it is still a good idea to check newspapers on a daily basis. Classified ads from many of the nation's prominent newspapers are listed online with www.careerpath.com.

Online Sources

Since online employment resources are expanding rapidly, you can start your job hunt by conducting a keyword search for employment resources on popular Internet search sites such as Yahoo! or Google. You should also visit the websites of the appropriate professional associations, which often maintain job banks and list other helpful resources; the American Dental Association, in particular, has an extensive network of job listings in its online classified section. Some sites, such as www.monster.com, let you post your résumé in addition to allowing you to search for jobs. Be careful about doing this if you're currently employed, as you may find that your employer is also browsing these sites!

Unsolicited Contact

A quick look through the phone book will give you an idea of the number of dental offices in your area. If there aren't too many, make a quick phone call to inquire about openings. You might get lucky and have one land in an office with a new, unadvertised opening. During the phone call, ask if you can send a résumé for the office to keep on file if there isn't a current opening available.

If a dentist you contact is not looking for an employee, ask him or her to pass your résumé on to a colleague who may be hiring. Dental supply representatives also are excellent resources. They visit offices on a routine basis and usually are knowledgeable about current employment situations. Dental supply reps are concerned with creating and maintaining goodwill, and most are happy to help.

Dental Placement Services

Most metropolitan areas have dental auxiliary placement services. Fee arrangements vary among agencies. Some charge the employer, some the employee, and some divide the placement fee between both parties. Most agencies are listed in the telephone directory or online, and many advertise in newspaper classified ads and in professional publications. If you decide to use one of these services, be sure you read and understand thoroughly the terms of any contracts into which you enter.

Temporary Employment Agencies

A temporary placement service is a company that provides employees to meet short-term needs. "Temps" may be needed on short notice for short periods of time, to substitute for a dental hygienist or assistant who is ill, for example, or for planned, longer periods, such as for a maternity leave or vacation. Many temporary dental care professionals have landed ideal permanent employment this way. You also get a chance to work closely with the staff and the dentist before making a permanent commitment.

Get Ready for the Interview

Finally, the last step to getting your new job is preparing for and acing the interview. There are a variety of excellent books that offer expert advice on all aspects of the interview process, and it would be well worth the investment if you purchase and study a few. These books offer tips about how to answer common interview questions, how to lead the interview, and how to make sure you get across what you want the interviewer to know about yourself.

While it is beyond the scope of this book to offer in-depth information about the interviewing process, there are a few key things you must do to make sure you're one of the top candidates. First of all, appearances are important in applying for a job in which you will be working with all kinds of people, so be sure to wear conservative dress, a suit if possible, and bring a fresh résumé, transcripts, or any other information in an attractive portfolio or briefcase. Promptness is important in any job situation, so plan to arrive a few minutes early to the interview. If you have to travel to a new community for the interview, allow plenty of time to locate the office. To show the prospective employer that you're interested in working for him or her, during the interview ask questions about the organization, its aims, and history. When you leave the interview, if you want to be considered for the position, state that you do.

After the interview, be sure to write a thank-you letter within one or two days. In your thank-you note, provide any additional information you were unable to work into the interview and reemphasize your interest in the position. Be prepared to repeat these steps until you have found the position and location that is right for you.

8

SETTING UP THE DENTIST'S OFFICE

SETTING UP AND establishing a successful dental practice is a fairly elaborate and involved process. Because it takes considerable time and money, it's best to be well educated and prepared in this area. Anyone who thinks they may be interested in working in a dental office should have some basic knowledge of what it takes to set one up. In this chapter, you'll read about the various components of the dental office, from equipment to employees.

General Practice Office

The most common professional setting for dentists, dental hygienists, and dental assistants is in a general practice office. In this setting, employees work as a team to provide the most efficient care for patients. Team members, including the dental and administrative assistants, work in various capacities to provide treatment.

Treatment is often preventive and usually addresses the relatively minor concerns of cavities, plaque, gingivitis, crowns, and cosmetic dentistry. The general practice office is typically located in an office building or in its own freestanding structure. More acute dentistry is often practiced in a hospital setting.

The general practice office tends to have a variety of assistive personnel. Assistants to one or more dentists include a dental hygienist, dental assistant, sometimes a laboratory technician, and often a receptionist or an administrative assistant. Duties of the dental hygienist and the assistant may overlap, but the dental hygienist tends to work independently in caring for the patient. The dental assistant, on the other hand, works directly with and under the supervision of the dentist. The receptionist answers phones, deals with the files, and completes paperwork. Chapter 2 describes the work of the dentist; Chapter 3 describes the duties of the support staff in the general practice office in more detail.

A Day at the Dentist's Office

This section will give you a better understanding of how the dental office team works together by taking you through a typical day at the office. For a more personal experience, you could contact a dentist in your area—maybe even your own!—and ask him or her if you can shadow, or spend time with, each of the various members of the dental care team for a day. Most people will be flattered that you're taking an interest in their occupation and will be more than happy to show you around. Just be sure to thank them repeatedly for their efforts, and come prepared with any questions you can think of to ask.

A receptionist or administrative assistant is the first person to welcome a patient into the dental office. As such, the receptionist must have a friendly and pleasant disposition to make the patient, who is undoubtedly nervous, feel at ease. If this is a first visit, either the dental assistant takes the patient's dental and medical history through an interview process or the receptionist gives the patient several forms with health-related questions to fill out. After the appropriate paperwork is done, the receptionist escorts the patient to a private room where he or she is introduced to the dental hygienist.

The hygienist works in an office, called the *operatory*, that contains a dental chair, the patient's chart, and equipment for cleaning teeth and taking X-rays. The dental hygienist, as with all team members, follows infection control procedures and wears disposable gloves and masks and protective eyewear when working on patients' teeth. The hygienist first takes X-rays of the patient's teeth to visualize cavities, plaque, and other problems. Then he or she performs a complete cleaning (prophylaxis), which includes removing the hardened material (calculus) from all surfaces of the teeth, cleaning with an electric brush, flossing, and providing a fluoride treatment. The hygienist will typically describe what is being done and give instructions about the best home care for healthy teeth. After the dental hygienist has finished the cleaning, the patient meets the dentist and dental assistant.

The dentist and dental assistant work as a team, and the dentist takes the lead during the entire examination. The dentist typically engages in some small talk with the patient to set him or her at ease. He or she asks if there are any questions or concerns and then examines the patient's entire mouth and looks at the radiographs. After that, the treatment is determined.

Treatment for the patient may consist of placement of a restoration (filling) in one or several teeth, construction of a denture to replace missing teeth, or extraction of a tooth that cannot be saved.

The dentist also checks for any indications of periodontal (gum) disease, signs of oral cancers, or need for orthodontic (alignment of teeth) or endodontic (root canal) therapy. Several appointments may be necessary to complete the treatment procedure. The dentist eventually pronounces the course of treatment a success and the patient hopefully leaves feeling pleased with the work.

While the dentist is performing the examination and treatment interventions, the assistant assembles and hands the necessary tools to the dentist. The patient is seated in a comfortable, adjustable chair that can be raised or lowered to allow the dentist and assistant to work conveniently. While the dentist will handle the more difficult interventions, the assistant or hygienist may perform part of the treatment.

The laboratory technician prepares the end results of the assistant and dentist's procedure. The technician follows the design and instructions to construct an individualized crown, bridge, or denture (prosthesis) that fits in the patient's mouth comfortably and matches the color of the patient's teeth. If the prosthesis isn't a perfect fit, the technician may have to make additional adjustments.

Before the dental team is even assembled and the dental office is in working order, the dentist must make several important decisions. Dentistry is a business, and, in many instances, the dentist has to acquire some business skills in addition to scientific knowledge. The following sections cover additional items dentists must consider when setting up their practices.

Office Design

More and more often, dentists must take great care and consideration in the design of the office space. It is the visual representation of the practice; as such, the environment must be one that is highly efficient, attractive, and stress reducing. This is so important that interior designers have set up businesses specializing in or focusing on dental office design. Soft lighting, warm paint tones, art, and aquariums all help set patients at ease as they wait to see the dentist. Each room in the dental office serves a specific function and will need more or less design, depending on the use of the space and whether it is open to patients.

Reception Room

The reception room should be especially attractive in appearance to welcome patients. It should contain comfortable chairs, reading material, storage for coats, and a device, such as door chimes, to signal when a patient enters.

Business Office

Files, desks, and computers are the standard equipment needed in the office, with space for appointment books, photocopier, telephones, and other items necessary for scheduling, paying bills, and discussing financial arrangements. This part of the office should be kept separate from the operatories.

Operatories

As stated earlier, the operatory is the room in which the dentist examines the patient. The number of operatories varies depending on the size of the dental practice, but for a smaller practice, two operatories are recommended. Each room will contain a dental chair, cabinet, sink, stools, and equipment area. The dental operatory should be designed in such a way that the dental team can easily conform with all infection control requirements. It should be an uncluttered space with good ventilation, and the floor covering should be easy to clean and free of seams. In fact, all surfaces in this room should be smooth and easy to clean and disinfect. As in other parts of the office, a pleasant, relaxing atmosphere should be created by the use of attractive color schemes and decorations.

Laboratory and Darkroom

One room can serve both laboratory and darkroom functions, unless the dentist plans to have a complete laboratory in which artificial teeth and other appliances are made. The laboratory should be near the operatories, have adequate plumbing, and include an area for the processing of film. The laboratory should be equipped with products for disinfection and sterilization of the dental office to meet current infection control recommendations. In addition, an area must be set aside for the safe disposal of waste materials.

Closets and Storage Space

The dental team should make sure that supplies and personal items are stored away from the view of the general public in closets or storage spaces. Dental files and records often take up considerable space, so having enough storage on hand will keep the office organized and tidy. When shopping for office space, the dentist should look for a place with enough storage to meet his or her needs and that of a growing practice.

Restroom

One restroom is usually sufficient, although some dentists prefer to have one for the patients and one for the dental team. This prevents the patient from wondering whether the dental team is practicing good hand-washing techniques. The restroom, as is usually the case, should be well lit and tidy.

Optional Rooms

For the new practitioner, the rooms just covered are all that is needed to set up a well-run and complete dental practice. For larger or more established operations, however, there are additional rooms that may prove beneficial to the practice. Having a private office, staff lounge, conference room, and additional operatories may make a larger practice more comfortable to work in. Of course, the office layout depends on the number of patients seen and the size of the practice.

Equipment and Services

Dentistry is unique in that a dentist must provide not only personal expertise, but also the physical equipment needed to practice. In contrast, a medical practitioner usually is associated with a hospital and can use the laboratory equipment available there. The dental office must include standard laboratory equipment, as well as darkroom, business office, reception room, and individual operatory areas, each one fully equipped with the latest advancements in dental machinery.

Obtaining the machinery and technology available to become a competitive dental practice is an expensive undertaking. Many new dentists decide to set up shop with an established dental team to forgo taking out large bank loans to finance the operation. For those who prefer to strike out on their own, used equipment is often available. The advantage of used equipment over new is the cost, which is one-fourth to one-half the price. However, new equipment requires less maintenance and often comes with a warranty that allows the purchaser to replace it if it's broken within a certain period of time. An established dental supplier can offer advice to those starting up a practice and help the dentist decide what kind of equipment is best for the budget and style of the office.

Location

The first thing a dental school graduate must do after receiving his or her license to practice is determine where to set up the dental practice. A location where a lot of people will see the office and one that isn't too close to competitors' offices is the safest bet.

In choosing a location for the office, a dentist may consider the following:

- Year-round climate and access to services
- Population and size of potential client base
- Whether the clientele will be families or persons of similar age and background
- Price of commercial space for setting up a practice
- Attractiveness of the space
- Visibility of the practice
- Location of the nearest competitor
- Number of competitors in the area

There are several ways to determine whether a potential site for a dental practice meets these criteria. While simply driving around an area can tell you a lot about the viability of setting up shop there, the local chamber of commerce can provide you with more details about competitors and real estate prices in the area. Many areas also have a local dental society that can be a good source of information. Be sure to read the publications of the American Dental Association, local dental supply houses, and financial institutions in the community. Finally, there are numerous books available to help you make an informed choice.

Creating the Dental Care Team

Every employee of the dental practice must be chosen with care because everyone will have some kind of interaction with the clientele; each member of the dental care team plays a part in creating a positive experience for the client. In addition, it costs between 100 and 300 percent of an employee's annual salary to replace him or her, making a hasty choice an expensive one. Whether you will be the interviewer or the interviewee, you are sure to find the following section about building a cohesive dental team valuable.

A small, start-up practice may consist of only the dentist and one other person who will act as receptionist, secretary, and dental assistant. This person must be adept at multitasking and be able to learn a variety of roles quickly. He or she must also have an impeccable record of not missing work. A person taking this kind of job may find working in such a practice unpleasant if he or she doesn't get along well with the dentist; or, he or she may find that the variety of tasks makes for an exciting day at the office.

Conversely, a larger office offers more social interaction with a range of coworkers, but also more confinement to a particular role or task. In a larger group setting, working as a team is vitally important. Creating a strong and positive group dynamic is largely the responsibility of the person in charge, usually the dentist; the first step is choosing employees whose personalities will complement each other. Similarly, it's important for prospective employees to either spend a day in the office observing the group dynamics before accepting the job, or at least speak with others in the office to get a sense of their level of job satisfaction.

When hiring a prospective employee, many employers want to know why that person left his or her previous position. If the candidate is a graduate applying for a first job out of school, this will not be an issue. For others who have had some experience, employers may spend more time trying to gauge whether the person left on good terms.

Several general traits are most valuable to employers. These include flexibility and an eagerness to learn and take on responsibilities. Working hours and responsibilities may vary because of emergency situations and because most dental offices are open on evenings and weekends. A flexible employee will be able to handle any kind of situation and in turn will be rewarded with raises and promotions.

Training Employees

Investing the time and effort into training employees thoroughly and properly from the beginning will pay off in the end. The result is a more efficient and effective office that is a pleasant place for clients to come to and for the dental staff to work in. There are several items to consider for making sure employees understand what is expected of them and that will help ensure that the office runs smoothly. They include the following:

- There should be written records of job descriptions, along with a procedures manual, available to employees.

Procedures should be outlined for each person on a daily, weekly, monthly, and annual basis.

- Employee benefits should be clearly defined: dental care, vacations, sick leave, salary and review, paid holidays, and medical care or pension plan.
- Staff meetings should be held regularly to formally discuss problems, allowing feedback from employees to influence changes in office procedures.

Prospective employees should inquire about the length of time dedicated to training someone in their position and whether the training will be done by the person who is leaving or someone else. Longer lengths of time and a person more experienced in the job are indicative of a higher-quality, more efficient and effective transition. This means that the new employee is less likely to be overwhelmed during this stressful time.

Communicating with Patients

Effective communication is necessary for delivering high-quality health care. Members of the dental team must be able to communicate well to assess a patient's concerns, acknowledge any contributing life events, and ease his or her anxiety. Various tools can be used to develop two-way communication between the dental staff and patients. Other health care providers, in fact, also employ many of these tools, which include the following:

- Explain the patient's treatment in a positive manner without technical terms. Be sure the patient understands the proposed treatment.

- Emphasize the benefits of treatment. Use radiographs, photographs, or other available visual aids to make a point.
- Carefully describe the risks or downsides of the treatment, including the physical and financial aspects.
- Ask the dental assistant to help with the explanation, especially with the details of appointment times, length of appointments, and any anesthesia to be given.
- During any treatment and procedure, explain what is being done to the patient and what tools are being used to reduce anxiety.
- Warn the patient if any procedure is going to be painful, and reassure him or her of the steps that will be taken to minimize the pain.

Following Up

Regular examinations and professional cleaning are necessary for achieving and maintaining good dental health. Most dentists recommend their patients come in for checkups every six months. Because this is fairly frequent in terms of preventive care measures, some type of recall system is generally helpful to clients, because they are reminded to make their appointments, and to dentists, because it ensures they will have steady work. One of the most effective and least costly recall systems is the postcard. Some computer programs can also be used, which prompts the receptionist or administrative assistant to call the patient to set up an appointment. Well-organized files should be set up so that each patient can be reminded two or more weeks before the next checkup is scheduled.

Insurance Plans

Many insurance plans now cover dental care, which means that a tremendous amount of paperwork is generated from dealing with insurance companies. Dentists should establish office procedures to handle the paperwork involved and separate insurance records from the dental files for easy reference. After the dentist provides treatment, he or she should keep copies of claims and any other items, such as radiographs, that are submitted to the insurance company. These records will be useful if an insurance company loses a claim.

A good dentist discusses the treatment plan and insurance benefits in detail with the patient. Many insurance plans will cover certain items, but not others. For example, a plan may cover metal fillings, but not porcelain ones. Because porcelain is less noticeable, many patients prefer it, but with aesthetics comes a higher price tag. The dental team must be informed about insurance plans and able to explain the nuances accurately to clients.

Recordkeeping

The person or persons in charge of the dental office administration creates and maintains files and records for billing, insurance forms, patient reminders, payroll expenses, and income taxes. Dentists can purchase any number of different organizational systems from dental supply stores to keep these records neat and tidy. Office administrators also maintain records of financial activity in a daily log that includes the list of patients, description of services provided, charges, payments, and balances due. In addition to financial records, they maintain an inventory of supplies and equipment, which must be kept current and accurate so that an assistant can order supplies well before they run out.

Patient files contain a record of treatments provided by the dentist. For a large or successful practice, these files may be extensive and take up significant space, so good organization is vital. The records typically include the following:

- Personal information, including type of insurance coverage
- Medical history with age, weight, height, diseases, medication, allergies, and physician's name
- Various diagnoses and treatment plans
- X-rays and photographs
- A financial record of payments

Professional Advisors

Although we previously stated that dentists must have a certain amount of business acumen to run a successful dental practice, this does not mean that they are able to handle all of the business-related issues that come up. In fact, dentists rely on a variety of professionals to help them set up and establish a successful practice. The following professional advisors help dentists keep their businesses running efficiently and well:

- **Accounting consultant.** This person creates bookkeeping systems and reviews annual records for tax purposes.
- **Insurance broker.** A qualified insurance broker meets with the dentist periodically to make sure his or her malpractice insurance is current and appropriate and to obtain health insurance for the dental care team.
- **Attorney.** An attorney—typically one that specialized in dental practices—handles tax advice, leasing contracts, and partnerships.
- **Investment counselor.** An experienced counselor provides seasoned judgment and guidance for making many types of investments, from stocks to upgrading facilities.

The Measure of Success

There are many benefits to entering the field of dental health. As a health care provider, the dental professional is well regarded in the community. Additionally, the monetary rewards are greater than those in many other fields, ensuring a measure of financial security. However, the greatest benefit comes from professional accomplishment and the satisfaction of providing a valuable service.

After all the preparation is made, the ultimate basis for a successful practice is your professional reputation and concern for patients. You will need to educate patients in oral health, communicate with them about their treatment, convey a sense of confidence in yourself and your practice, follow through with your concern, and, most important, provide the highest quality of care. In return, you will enjoy a stable and reliable clientele, who may also recruit others to your practice.

9

THE FUTURE OF DENTISTRY

WHAT IS THE future of dentistry? The future of dentistry is as bright and energetic as a newly whitened smile. Opportunities abound for those with people skills, scientific knowledge, a strong work ethic, and an interest in working with cutting-edge treatments and state-of-the-art technology. Some of the techniques and treatments of the future may surprise you; at the very least they are sure to excite you. While many of the techniques discussed in this chapter have been developed and approved by the Food and Drug Administration (www.fda.gov), they are not widely used by the majority of dentists in practice because they are so new. Are you ready to lend your talents and brainpower to the revolutionary future of dentistry?

A Look Ahead

Experts predict that the occurrence of decay will continue to be reduced as emphasis on preventive dentistry is increased, and that periodontal or gum disease will be a continuing problem that will need to be treated. Better materials are being developed to restore (fill) teeth and seal them against caries (tooth decay) and disease. Studies are under way to measure the role of specific foods and how they affect the caries process that produces decay. In dental education, curriculums in dental schools are are being revised so as to respond to these changes, and there is greater focus on patient care.

In addition, in the future, scientists, researchers, and practitioners alike will be looking more closely at the relationship between oral disease and patients' overall or systemic health. Current research indicates that inflammation and bacteria found in oral infections may contribute to a variety of systemic conditions, including cardiovascular and pulmonary disease, low-birth-weight infants and premature birth, osteoporosis, diabetes, and several other chronic, degenerative diseases. Many schools require recent dental health records of students before allowing them to enter, as good oral health is a positive indicator of good general health. If there is indeed a strong, direct connection between oral health and overall health, the scope of dental practice may broaden dramatically.

New Technology in Dentistry

Dentistry, with its associated careers, is a changing profession. As in many other scientific and health-related fields, advances in science and technology have led to new concepts of care. For example, lasers are used to remove tooth decay, and computers can be programmed to design precise crowns to fit teeth. Many types of implant devices hold crowns in place. As people take better care of their bodies, they are working harder to maintain healthy teeth, and some of this may include vaccines in the future. This section describes just some of the many new and exciting developments in the world of dentistry.

New "Drills"

The squealing and screeching, imposing, metal drills that are commonplace in dental offices may soon have a softer, more appealing appearance and function. The new tools do not have a metal drill bit; instead, they use a high-powered spray of sandlike material to remove cavities. While some dentists have caught on to the new tools, which are approved by the American Dental Association and the Food and Drug Administration (FDA), they are not yet widespread in the United States.

Better X-Rays

There are many ways in which a digital X-ray outperforms the standard one. A digital X-ray is an X-ray taken with a standard X-ray machine, which then exposes and transmits the image to a computer. The digital X-ray only uses 10 percent as much radiation to make an exposure as the traditional X-ray. Technicians can also manipulate digital images, infusing contrasts and changing the views, which help make for a better picture of the oral structures.

Working Fillings and Stronger Teeth

In the advanced research stage are fillings that not only fill a hole in the tooth, but also are busy fighting bacteria and other tooth-damaging elements. Scientists are working on fillings that release calcium and phosphate ions when they come in contact with acids from tooth bacteria. Animal studies show that the ions prevent and repair cavities, but human clinical studies are not yet complete. In addition, a similar material will soon be on the market for braces and will help prevent cavities from forming underneath difficult-to-clean hardware.

Similarly, a new toothpaste, which is still in the market-testing phase, has been developed that builds stronger teeth. Enamelon toothpaste remineralizes tooth enamel, which hardens the tooth and results in fewer cavities. It works by using soluble calcium, phosphate, and fluoride to prevent cavities from forming in the first place. It also appears to reverse early stages of tooth decay and decrease tooth sensitivity.

Finally, researchers are working on something that could eliminate the need for much of the new technology presented in this chapter—a cavity vaccine. Although human clinical trials are not yet under way, animal studies have shown promise for the vaccine, which strengthens and stimulates the immune system to fight the cause of cavities (bacteria), thus preventing them from forming. The vaccine would be administered to children along with their regular course of vaccines and immunizations.

Implants and Lab-Grown Teeth

Implant dentistry and even lab-grown teeth may replace dentures as the treatment of choice for lost and missing teeth. Implants have been around for some time now and are becoming increasingly popular choices for replacing teeth. Dentures simply do not have the longevity of implants, and they require constant maintenance and periodic replacement. Dentures also are removable and less sturdy in the mouth. Implants, on the other hand, once they are firmly established in place, can last a lifetime. Titanium, a lightweight, incredibly strong material that is also used in artificial joint replacement surgeries, is the preferred metal to use in implants.

In the future, patients may grow their own replacement teeth from tooth buds. Isolated stem cells that form into dentin and enamel may be bioengineered to grow into teeth. The idea is that with the application of proteins to these specific cells, roots will grow into a jaw and dentin and enamel will cover the roots to form a tooth. Already scientists have formed crowns made of dentin and enamel in animal studies, although a whole tooth has yet to be formed.

Insurance and Dental Health Care Access

Improving access to dental health care will increasingly become a concern. Although most large employers offer health insurance benefits to their workers, only about half offer dental insurance. In fact, while the number of people with dental benefits nationwide increased over the past several years, two out of three full-time employees working for small businesses still do not have dental insurance. Currently, one hundred million Americans lack this coverage, thus private dental insurance payments account for a significant percentage of the national expenditure for dental care. For a person paying out-of-pocket, dental care can be quite expensive, which limits individuals from seeking regular dental care.

Health Care Access

As individuals, and through professional associations, dentists, hygienists, and assistants have worked to promote oral health for everyone. In the past, a variety of large-scale programs has been successful in treating and preventing dental disease, including:

- Fluoridation of community water supplies
- National dental health programs for children
- Placement programs and efforts to bring dentists into the small communities

- Provision of dental care for children within Medicaid and senior citizens within Medicare

However, large groups of people still do not receive dental care: the poor, elderly, handicapped, homebound, and institutionalized.

Nonprofit organizations are attempting to improve the opportunity for some of these people to receive dental care. Children receive oral health education and preventive services right in the schools. A community effort in New York State provides and equips a dental van in which dentists and assistants travel to treat children. In North Dakota, the Fargo-Moorhead dental community organized a clinic made up of fifty-eight dentists and oral surgeons who donate their time to relieve pain for indigent patients. Dental society programs supply dentures at cost to elderly persons, and treatment is given to those who don't need dentures. Several dental groups offer reduced fees for persons sixty-five years and older.

Since 1975 the National Foundation of Dentistry for the Handicapped (www.nfdh.org) has worked to address the dental needs of those who are not receiving care through several programs: the Campaign of Concern, Dental House Calls, and the Donated Dental Services program. The Campaign of Concern focuses on the mentally handicapped and others with developmental disabilities. It emphasizes teaching oral hygiene skills, diagnosing disease, and helping patients gain access to dental care by either arranging for their transportation to the dental office or scheduling volunteer dentists to make house calls. Dental House Calls is specifically aimed at securing dental treatment for those whose disabilities restrict them to their homes or long-term-care facilities. The program includes a van with portable dental equipment for dentists. The Donated Dental Services program involves matching volunteer dentists with the indigent elderly, handicapped, mentally ill, and homeless who cannot pay for care. These programs and others show the commitment of professionals in the dental health care field.

Governmental and organizational efforts are under way to make dental heath care more affordable to the masses. For example, the Massachusetts Dental Society offers the Dentistry for All program that puts consumers in touch with dentists who treat qualifying patients at reduced fees. Some state departments of health are also offering tuition reimbursement for dental students in exchange for a commitment to working with an underserved population, such as those living in rural areas. The federal government, as part of the Healthy People 2010 initiatives, has created an Oral Health Toolkit designed to increase the public's oral health and quality of life and to decrease oral health disparities. The tool kit is a guide offering advice, methods, resources, and examples of successful efforts to help communities plan, implement, and evaluate their oral health efforts. Oral Health America (www.oralhealthamerica.org) is a nonprofit organization with an extensive network of programs ranging from the National Sealant Alliance, which pledges to provide one million dental sealants to approximately 225,000 children by 2010, to the National Spit Tobacco Education Program, which educates people, especially young people, about the dangers of spit tobacco use and helps users quit.

While these efforts are certainly a start, it is up to the new and future dentists to continue to think of ways to make regular dental checkups as important a part of the public's preventive care efforts as vaccines and regular doctor visits. Perhaps the best way to do this is to integrate dentistry into primary care. As a future dental health professional, it will be up to you to make this kind of grand social change.

Career opportunities are available in the programs just discussed and many other nonprofit, governmental, and charitable organizations for concerned persons who want to work with all types of patients, increasing access to dental health services. As dental health increases in importance in the general population, more funding for assistance programs will become available, creating job opportunities for those willing to lend a hand. Some even find that volunteering without pay brings numerous rewards in itself.

Women in Dentistry

Traditionally, the various positions in dentistry have placed men and women in certain roles; however, these roles are changing. Men have been dominant in the professional role of dentists, women have been hygienists and assistants, and men have been in the majority as laboratory technicians. The most dramatic change is the increased percentage of women becoming dentists. The percentage of first-year enrollment by women in dental schools increased from 17.5 percent in 1979, to 33.2 percent in 1988, to 50 percent early in 2000.

The increase in the number of women entering U.S. dental schools is similar to the increasing number of women in prominent and varied positions in all health care fields, which is a result of the changing status of female health care providers. The older population of baby boomers grew up with ideas of women's right to equal pay and position, as have their children, which makes them less likely to shy away from seeing a female health care provider. These changing attitudes will continue to open doors for female dentists.

While most dentists are owners or share in the ownership of the practice in which they treat patients, fewer women own practices than their male counterparts. Similarly, according to the U.S.

Department of Health, women tend to earn less practicing dentistry than men. This may be due, in part, to the fact that women, the traditional primary caregivers, work more part-time hours so that they can raise young children. One government study showed that nearly 50 percent of women in dentistry work no more than the equivalent of two days a week, the primary reason being to raise a family. The independence of the profession permits a more flexible schedule for family concerns for both men and women, although women tend to use it more because they tend to be the primary caregivers. In the future, some of these disparities can be addressed by an increasing attitude shift toward a more realistic work-life balance for men and women, more flexible working patterns, and greater access to continuing education for those who take time off.

Unfortunately, dental schools have a long way to go to achieve equality for women in academia. According to the U.S. Department of Health, dentistry has become an increasingly popular career for women, and by 2005 there were more women than men graduating from dental schools; yet few women are in positions of power within universities. For example, women are more likely to be instructors or assistant professors while men are more likely to be associate or full professors. In addition, while 60 percent of U.S. dental schools had women in department chair positions, only 12.7 percent of them had appointed women as deans or interim or acting deans, a disproportionately low number. Dental school students and organizations must use their influence to change these statistics so that those setting school curricula are representative of the student body and future dentistry leaders.

The distribution of men and women among specific professional occupations is less pronounced today than it was twenty years ago;

the same is true for the roles of dental assistants and hygienists, typically female roles that have increasingly become more integrated by men. As people in these positions assume more responsibilities and independence, the work is becoming more autonomous, rewarding, and fulfilling for both men and women. These two careers, plus that of the laboratory technician, are open to those who are qualified—regardless of gender.

Minorities in Dentistry

The number of students from ethnic minority groups has steadily increased in all areas of dental training over the past twenty years; unfortunately, there's still a long way to go. While the United States has become more diverse with minorities making up 25 percent of the population, only 14 percent of currently practicing dentists are minorities, and minorities make up only 11 percent of students in dental programs. One study indicated that this might be due, in part, to the fact that minority groups are not as likely to be groomed from a young age to consider dental health care as a career option. In addition, minority students were more hesitant about going into debt to finance their education than their white counterparts. Potential efforts to address this problem could include greater outreach activities for recruiting minority undergraduates and high school students and distributing information about scholarships and grants. In summary, there remain gender and ethnic barriers in dentistry, making achieving positions of greater power and prestige less likely for women and minorities.

The good news is that there are a variety of groups and organizations currently dedicated to promoting the advancement of minorities in the dental health care field. One example is the Hispanic Dental Association (www.hdassoc.org), which, among other things, offers scholarships to help fund education at all levels. Another is the Society of American Indian Dentists (www.aaip .com/said), a group that encourages American Indian youth to pursue a career in dentistry and provides assistance to students who are interested in the profession of dentistry. The American Dental Education Association (www.adea.org) publishes *Opportunities for Minority Students in United States Dental Schools*, an all-in-one guide designed to attract minorities to dentistry. A detailed online search using a variety of keywords and soliciting the help of a career counselor should help you find a wealth of information.

Geographic Location

The density of dentists by region and state is something to consider when you're deciding where to begin practicing. Currently, large metropolitan areas and small towns are often saturated with dentists, while rural and medium-sized communities are in need of dental care providers. Dentists willing to relocate to these areas of need will have the best chance of establishing a successful practice. Because this information is ever changing, you should look up the most recent information by doing an online search or contacting the appropriate government agency. Statistics on the shortage of health professionals by state and county are available by contacting the Division of Shortage Designation, Bureau of Primary Health Care, Health Resources and Services Administration, 4350 East-West Highway, 9th Floor, Room 9-1D3, Bethesda, MD 20814.

A Bright Future

As you've learned from reading this book, those who enter the field of dentistry have a bright future. Opportunities abound, the compensation is excellent, and dental health care personnel work in increasingly diverse settings. Conducting careful and thorough research using a variety of resources will ensure that you're well equipped to begin your dental health care studies. Good luck finding the career of your dreams!

Dental Schools

U.S. Schools

The following schools are members of the American Dental Education Association.

Alabama

University of Alabama, School of Dentistry
www.dental.uab.edu

Arizona

Arizona School of Dentistry and Oral Health
http://asdoh.atsu.edu

California

Loma Linda University, School of Dentistry
www.llu.edu/llu/dentistry

University of California–Los Angeles, School of Dentistry
www.dent.ucla.edu

University of California–San Francisco, School of Dentistry
www.ucsf.edu

University of the Pacific, Arthur A. Dugoni School of Dentistry
http://dental.pacific.edu

University of Southern California, School of Dentistry
www.usc.edu/hsc/dental

Colorado

University of Colorado, Health Sciences Center
www.uchsc.edu/sod

Connecticut

University of Connecticut, School of Dental Medicine
http://sdm.uchc.edu

District of Columbia

Howard University, College of Dentistry
www.howard.edu

Florida

Nova Southeastern University, College of Dental Medicine
http://dental.nova.edu

University of Florida, College of Dentistry
www.dental.ufl.edu

Georgia

Medical College of Georgia, School of Dentistry
www.mcg.edu/sod

Illinois

Southern Illinois University, School of Dental Medicine
www.siue.edu/sdm

University of Illinois–Chicago, College of Dentistry
http://dentistry.uic.edu

Indiana

Indiana University, School of Dentistry
www.iusd.iupui.edu

Iowa

The University of Iowa, College of Dentistry
www.dentistry.uiowa.edu

Kentucky

University of Kentucky, College of Dentistry
www.mc.uky.edu/dentistry

University of Louisville, School of Dentistry
www.dental.louisville.edu/dental

Louisiana

Louisiana State University, School of Dentistry
www.lsusd.lsuhsc.edu

Maryland

University of Maryland–Baltimore, College of Dental Surgery
www.dental.umaryland.edu

Massachusetts

Boston University, Goldman School of Dental Medicine
http://dentalschool.bu.edu

Harvard University, School of Dental Medicine
www.hsdm.med.harvard.edu

Tufts University, School of Dental Medicine
www.tufts.edu/dental

Michigan

University of Detroit Mercy, School of Dentistry
www.udmercy.edu/dental

University of Michigan, School of Dentistry
www.dent.umich.edu

Minnesota

University of Minnesota, School of Dentistry
www.dentistry.umn.edu

Mississippi

University of Mississippi, School of Dentistry Medical Center
http://dentistry.umc.edu

Missouri

University of Missouri–Kansas City, School of Dentistry
www.umkc.edu/dentistry

Nebraska

Creighton University, School of Dentistry
http://cudental.creighton.edu

University of Nebraska, Medical Center, College of Dentistry
www.unmc.edu/dentistry

New Jersey

University of Medicine and Dentistry, New Jersey Dental School
www.umdnj.edu

New York

Columbia University Medical Center, School of Dental
and Oral Surgery
http://dental.columbia.edu

New York University, College of Dentistry
www.nyu.edu/dental

State University of New York–Buffalo, School of Dental Medicine
www.sdm.buffalo.edu

State University of New York–Stony Brook, School of
Dental Medicine
www.hsc.stonybrook.edu/dental

North Carolina

University of North Carolina, School of Dentistry
www.dent.unc.edu

Ohio

Case Western Reserve University, School of Dental Medicine
www.case.edu/dental/site/main.html

Ohio State University, College of Dentistry
www.dent.ohio-state.edu

Oklahoma

University of Oklahoma, College of Dentistry
http://dentistry.ouhsc.edu

Oregon

Oregon Health Science University, School of Dentistry
www.ohsu.edu/sod/admissions

Pennsylvania

Temple University, School of Dentistry
www.temple.edu/dentistry

University of Pennsylvania, School of Dental Medicine
www.dental.upenn.edu

University of Pittsburgh, School of Dental Medicine
www.dental.pitt.edu

South Carolina

Medical University of South Carolina, College of Dental Medicine
www.gradstudies.musc.edu/dentistry/dental.html

Tennessee

Meharry Medical College, School of Dentistry
http://dentistry.mmc.edu

University of Tennessee, College of Dentistry
www.utmem.edu/dentistry

Texas

Texas A & M University System, Baylor College of Dentistry
www.tambcd.edu

University of Texas, Health Science Center, Houston Dental Branch
www.db.uth.tmc.edu

University of Texas, Health Science Center, San Antonio Dental
School
www.dental.uthscsa.edu

Virginia

Virginia Commonwealth University, School of Dentistry
www.dentistry.vcu.edu

Washington

University of Washington, School of Dentistry
www.dental.washington.edu

West Virginia

West Virginia University, School of Dentistry
www.hsc.wvu.edu/sod

Wisconsin

Marquette University, School of Dentistry
www.dental.mu.edu

Canadian Schools

The following schools are also members of the American Dental
Education Association.

Alberta

University of Alberta–Edmonton, Faculty of Medicine and Oral
    Health Sciences
www.dent.ualberta.ca

British Columbia

University of British Columbia–Vancouver, Faculty of Dentistry
www.dentistry.ubc.ca

Manitoba

University of Manitoba–Winnepeg, Faculty of Dentistry
www.umanitoba.ca/dentistry

Montreal

McGill University–Québec, Faculty of Dentistry
www.mcgill.ca/dentistry

Université Laval–Québec, Faculté de médecine dentaire
www.fmd.ulaval.ca

Université de Montréal–Faculté de médecine dentaire
www.medent.umontreal.ca

Nova Scotia

Dalhousie University–Halifax, Faculty of Dentistry
www.dentistry.dal.ca

Ontario

University of Toronto, Faculty of Dentistry
www.utoronto.ca/dentistry

University of Western Ontario–London, School of Dentistry
www.fmd.uwo.ca/dentistry

Saskatchewan

University of Saskatchewan–Saskatoon, College of Dentistry
www.usask.ca/dentistry

Appendix B

Professional Associations

The following organizations can provide you with a wealth of information. Contact those that are specific to your particular professional goals.

Dental Assistants

American Dental Assistants Association
www.dentalassistant.org

Dental Assisting National Board, Inc.
www.danb.org

National Dental Assistants Association
www.ndaonline.org

Dental Hygienists

American Dental Hygienists' Association
www.adha.org

National Dental Hygienists Association
www.ndhaonline.org

Dentists

Academy of Dentistry International
www.adint.org

Academy of Dentistry for Persons with Disabilities
www.scdonline.org

Academy of Laser Dentistry
www.laserdentistry.org

Academy of Operative Dentistry
http://operativedentistry.com

Academy of Prosthodontics
www.academyprosthodontics.org

Academy for Sports Dentistry
www.sportsdentistry-iasd.org

Alliance of the American Dental Association
www.allianceada.org

American Academy of Cosmetic Dentistry
www.aacd.com

American Academy of Dental Group Practice
www.aadgp.org

American Academy of Esthetic Dentistry
www.estheticacademy.org

American Academy of Fixed Prosthodontics
www.fixedprosthodontics.org

American Academy of Gnathologic Orthopedics
www.aago.com

American Academy of Implant Dentistry
www.aaid-implant.org

American Academy of Pediatric Dentistry
www.aapd.org

American Academy of Periodontology
www.perio.org

American Academy of Restorative Dentistry
www.restorativeacademy.com

American Association for Dental Research
www.dentalresearch.org

American Association of Dental Schools
www.irandental.org/dental_schools.htm

American Association of Endodontists
www.aae.org

American Association of Hospital Dentists
www.scdonline.org

American Association of Oral and Maxillofacial Surgeons
www.aaoms.org

American Association of Orthodontists
www.aaomembers.org

American Association of Public Health Dentistry
www.aaphd.org

American Dental Association
www.ada.org

American Student Dental Association
www.asdanet.org

National Dental Association
www.ndaonline.org

Laboratory Technicians

National Association of Dental Laboratories
www.nadl.org

National Board for Certification in Dental Laboratory Technology
www.nbccert.org

Veterinary Dentists

American Society of Veterinary Dental Technicians
www.asvdt.org

American Veterinary Dental College
www.avdc.org

Veterinary Oral Health Council
www.vohc.org